CLEAR ROUND

OTHER BOOKS IN THE PONY LIBRARY INCLUDE

PONY CLUB CAMP
PONY CLUB TEAM
ONE DAY EVENT
WISH FOR A PONY
CARGO OF HORSES
NO ENTRY
STOLEN PONIES
WE HUNTED HOUNDS
RIDERS FROM AFAR
HORSES AT HOME
I WANTED A PONY
RIDING WITH THE LYNTONS
FIRST PONY
JACKY JUMPS TO THE TOP
STABLE TO LET
PONIES ON THE HEATHER
THE SURPRISE RIDING CLUB
A PONY FOR TWO
AFRAID TO RIDE
REBEL PONY
THE TRICK JUMPERS
A PONY FOR SALE
WE RODE TO THE SEA

COLLINS PONY LIBRARY

CLEAR ROUND

Pamela MacGregor-Morris

COLLINS
LONDON & GLASGOW

First printed in this new edition 1973

ISBN 0 00 164321 5

PRINTED AND MADE IN GREAT BRITAIN BY
WILLIAM COLLINS SONS AND CO. LTD.
LONDON AND GLASGOW

CONTENTS

". . . And vaulted with such ease into his seat
As if an angel dropped down from the clouds
To turn and wind a fiery Pegasus
And witch the world with noble horseman-
ship."

(William Shakespeare).

CHAPTER I

ROTTEN ROW

AS THE bus trundled its way along Piccadilly, stopping interminably at every red light, Fiona Jamieson sat in the offside front seat and stared blankly out of the window.

She was on her way home from a class visit to the British Museum, but the afternoon spent among the treasures of ancient Egypt was already pushed away into a back recess of her mind. She scarcely even registered the scene that lay below her—hotels and restaurants, the exclusive hatters, the motor-car showrooms with their rows of gleaming limousines and the people scurrying to and fro.

Only when they rounded Hyde Park Corner did she show any interest in her surroundings. Suddenly her grey eyes grew eager and her slim body tensed as she searched Rotten Row for its horses and riders.

It was a drizzly day, and the only people to have ventured into the park for a ride were two rather large young women, uninspiring to a degree, bumping along astride a pair of accommodating but very plain horses; but to this one bemused spectator they symbolised all the glorious figures, resplendent in rich costumes, who had disported themselves in the past on their fiery thoroughbreds along the *Route des Rois*.

For Fiona, Rotten Row was the only interesting place in the whole of dreary London. She gazed wistfully upon the commonplace riders and their underbred mounts, and then searched the sandy, tree-lined ride for more. Soon however, the buildings obscured the Park from her sight and she sank back in her seat, put her hands deep in the pockets of her school raincoat, and resumed her day-dream until the bus arrived at her stop in Sloane Street.

Fiona had developed what her family referred to as her "horse fixation" at an early age, and for no apparent reason. Brought up in London, she had little opportunity to indulge her equestrian tastes, but the bulk of her reading matter had for years consisted of pony books. They were, for the most part, atrociously written and they bore a strong similarity to one another, but they had at least the merit of being full of information about ponies and their care, and she had accumulated it voraciously.

Her room was a veritable temple to the horse. Its walls were covered with pictures of the noble animal, cut out of magazines or torn off calendars and then painstakingly framed.

Everywhere one turned there were bits and spurs and horse brasses, picked up in antique and saddlers' shops, and a regular cavalry of china models adorned her mantlepiece.

Her favourite articles of clothing were her jodhpurs, which had been bought ready-made and were hopelessly baggy around the knees; a tweed coat, cut far too short, which she called her "hacking jacket"; a yellow tie, ornamented with a riot of horses' heads, foxes' masks and hunting whips which she secured to her shirt by means of a horse-head pin; and a black velvet cap which remained on her head thanks to a piece of black elastic which passed under her chin. Even now she was saving up for what she considered to be the finishing touch to the outfit, a pair of jodhpur boots with elastic sides.

A couple of years before, her godmother, Aunt Helen, who lived in Aberdeenshire, had, with the best intentions in the world, encouraged Fiona's preoccupation with the equine species with a birthday present which took the form of a course of lessons at the local riding school in Pelham Place. It was, had she but known it, a fatal move.

Every Saturday morning thereafter, Fiona bumped around Rotten Row on a solid cob, towed along by an estimable lady called Miss Dodd astride a superannuated hunter. Miss Dodd was a kindly soul, and she must have been extremely fond of both children and horses, for she only barely made enough from her riding lessons to keep herself and the stable full of old nags.

Fiona was encouraged to arrive early for her lessons and to remain helping in the stables afterwards. Miss Dodd, proprietress and chief instructress—indeed, the only instructress—was her own staff, with the exception of one aged groom who had seen better days in private service, and any voluntary help that could be enlisted was very welcome.

Fiona therefore filled hay-nets and water buckets, cleaned tack, groomed the six quiet animals and talked horse incessantly. Gradually her whole being came to revolve around the Pelham Place stables. Miss Dodd took her to see the Royal International Horse Show and the "Horse of the Year" Show at Wembley, and lent her any number of horse books—not pony books this time, but highly technical works with titles like "An Introduction to Dressage" and "The Forward Seat" which Fiona read avidly.

Miss Dodd, in actual fact, had never done more than glance through any of these treatises, which she had bought very cheaply second-hand because she felt that she ought to own them; but nothing would have dragged from her the confession that she could not quote them virtually word for word.

Truth to tell, her knowledge of both horses and riding was simply basic, but to Fiona she was the fount of all knowledge, the high priestess of the horse. If the opinions she expressed were sometimes the direct opposite of the theories which Fiona had absorbed from the borrowed books, then the books were not as accurate as they should have been.

Fiona's family viewed her "horsiness", as they called it, at first with amusement, later with concern, and finally, when she announced her intention of devoting her life to the cause, with consternation. Her brother Miles christened her "Miss Horse", and her father occasionally addressed her likewise. Her mother, however, refused to treat so lightly what she regarded as a serious situation. She had lost her nerve once and for all when she fell from a cousin's pony as a child. Now she disapproved on principle of what she termed "the horsy set". She found riding clothes unfeminine and hunting cruel, and she was even so unwise as to remark, in Fiona's hearing, that she thought that horses had stupid faces. Her daughter, to whom the horse was the most exquisite of all God's creatures, thereupon decided that she and her family had absolutely nothing in common.

On this particular afternoon she got off the bus and walked slowly home. Uppermost in her mind was the thought that in less than a month she would be leaving school and that, apart from horses, there was nothing in the world that she wanted to do. Various friends of hers planned to be doctors, nurses, models and secretaries, but none of these things was for her.

She opened the front door and went upstairs to the drawing room, hoping devoutly that the conversation would steer clear of her future.

"Darling!" cried her mother, a pretty woman who had taken every precaution against her hair turning grey or her figure spreading, "I've got some wonderful news for you! Your Aunt Helen's in London and she's coming to spend the night—and I've put your name down for the best secretarial college in London!"

Fiona's heart sank. It was starting again already.

"She'd much rather be a riding instructress, you know!" bantered Miles from the depths of the sofa.

"I'd make an awfully bad secretary," Fiona declared.

"Well, never mind, we can discuss it later," said her father, whose waistline—or lack of it—proclaimed him to be something fairly successful in the City. "Come and have a cup of tea while it's still hot."

"Surely the height of your ambition is not just to be a groom?" went on Mrs. Jamieson. "Anyone can do that kind of work."

"And anyone can pound a typewriter—that's what the biggest idiots I know are planning to do," said Fiona. "Besides, a riding instructress is not the same thing as a groom."

"Well, I simply don't understand you. Liking horses is one thing, but wanting to devote your entire life to them is quite another. You'll end up like that frightful Miss Dodd you seem to admire so much. I ask you, what sort of a life does she lead?"

"You'd be an old maid into the bargain, I expect," taunted Miles. "Hands in your pockets and straw in your hair and nothing to talk about but hocks and spavins. Poor old Fiona—what a dismal future to look forward to!"

Fiona flushed, despite herself. She could not help knowing that she was slim and chestnut-haired and attractive, and she did not relish the prospect of turning into a Miss Dodd, who was built like a battleship and had all the coats to her sensible tweed suits cut like riding coats so that she could wear them with a skirt or with jodhpurs, as occasion demanded.

"Let's drop the subject for now," suggested Mr. Jamieson. "Perhaps your Aunt Helen will be able to convince you that there are more pleasant and suitable occupations for young women than teaching children how not to fall off their ponies."

Fiona knew that it was not the slightest use to

try and explain to her family that there was more to riding than the mere act of sitting on a pony. Nor would they ever realise that equitation, at its highest, is an art. But, later in the evening, she found that she had a staunch ally in her godmother.

Aunt Helen was a splendid person. She considered a country life to be the only one worth living, and she lived it to the fullest. Her entrance hall on winter evenings was practically carpeted with elegant fawn deerhounds, lying sprawled in front of an enormous log fire. She was an avid gardener and the chairman of the local Women's Institute; she ran a company of Girl Guides and she canvassed with unabated enthusiasm for each successive Conservative candidate. She arranged the flowers in the village church and she was an accomplished fly fisherman and a first-class shot. Fiona held her in the highest esteem and affection.

Aunt Helen did not consider that Fiona was proposing to throw her life away. Far from it.

"Some friends of mine sent their daughter to a marvellous place in the Cotswolds—Wellesley Hall, at Littlebury, where the girls have to take French conversation, needlework and domestic science with their riding. They're terribly pleased with her. Before she went there she was positively immersed in horses and thought and talked of literally nothing else. Now she's a most attractive young woman with a lot of other interests. I'm sure that's just the place to send Fiona."

Aunt Helen was a very persuasive woman, and by the end of the evening she had convinced the Jamiesons that a year at Littlebury would be the best thing in the world for their daughter. She had also telephoned and found that Wellesley Hall would have a vacancy in the autumn, and had arranged for Fiona's parents to go down and see the place and to meet the owners the next weekend.

Fiona herself was in a complete whirl, but she went to bed that night happier than she had been for weeks, and fell asleep on the crest of a wave of optimism. Thanks to her godmother it really seemed as though life was going to be fun after all.

The following morning she rushed over to the stables to tell Miss Dodd about it. Rather to her surprise that lady, who was inclined to be impatient with things that she did not understand or approve of, was not terribly enthusiastic.

"I can't really see the point of mixing horses with cooking and needlework, my dear," she said. "I'm not in the least domesticated myself."

She spoke with some pride, as if lack of domesticity were in itself a virtue. Looking around at the general untidiness that prevailed in the flat over the stables where Miss Dodd lived alone with a snappy hunt terrier, Fiona was not at all sure that it was. She was devoted to this large, good-natured woman but for the first time she realised, almost subconsciously, that perhaps her idol might have feet of clay.

CHAPTER II

Wellesley Hall

Wellesley Hall was a lovely old Queen Anne house built of Cotswold stone, which time had mellowed to a greyish yellow. It stood in its own grounds just outside the village of Littlebury and it was, in fact, Colonel and Mrs. Anstruthers' family home. The house was too large and expensive to run for them to be able to afford to keep it up on the Colonel's Army pension, so they had turned it into a riding school combined with a finishing school, in order that they themselves might go on living there.

Colonel Bill Anstruther, a former cavalryman, was short and wiry with a small moustache and an engaging sense of humour. He drove his Land-Rover into Meltonham one rainy evening in late September and picked up Fiona and her luggage at the railway station. In the back of his vehicle lay a soaking wet, rough-coated lurcher which drew away from Fiona disdainfully when she tried to make friends with him.

"Don't mind Fly—he's a bit of a one-man dog, I'm afraid," said his owner with a note of pride in his voice which the owners of one-man dogs can never quite disguise. "Have you done much riding?"

"Well, not an *awful* lot," admitted Fiona cautiously. She knew from the books she had read that it was a fatal mistake to admit to very much in the way of either knowledge or ability where horses were concerned. If it turned out that she knew more than they expected, then the Anstruthers would be agreeably surprised. If not, then at least she would not have made herself look foolish by pretending to an experience which she did not in fact possess.

"Never mind," he said consolingly. "That's why you're coming to us. How's your French?"

"Not very brilliant," confessed Fiona.

He laughed. "Nor is mine! However, that's not my department. Mademoiselle takes care of that, and my wife looks after the cooking and sewing you'll have to do. I suppose you hate them both?"

Fiona smiled and nodded, and he smiled back at her.

"Oh well, that's nothing new—they all do. You'll enjoy your riding, though. We've got some good horses, all of them different. I think you'll agree that they are a far cry from the usual riding-school animals, and we have a lot of fun with them. Done any hunting?"

"No, but I'm longing to."

"And so you shall, as soon as the season starts.

Well, here we are. I hope you'll enjoy your stay with us."

The Land-Rover turned in through high, wrought-iron gates between stone pillars, to the right of which lay a round, lodge house, and they drove along the gravelled drive which wound through the park to the house. Close to the wooden fence stood a little group of three or four horses, gazing at them with mild interest. The Colonel slowed down as he passed them.

"Those are our young horses," he announced. "You'll have to help us break them in, in due course."

Fiona's heart leapt with delight. She feasted her eyes on the youngsters, and one of them, a big bay colt, as handsome as a painting by Munnings, stared straight back at her.

"What is that bay horse?" she asked.

"He's a three-year-old, coming four, that I bought last year in Ballinasloe Fair in Ireland. As a matter of fact, he's rather a disappointment. Funny-tempered animal, and we haven't been able to make much progress with him so far."

Fiona was fascinated. She felt a strange, inexplicable bond with the problem horse. Somehow, it was as if he had flung out a challenge to her, and already she had decided to accept it.

"The other horses are all stabled," said the Colonel, driving on up to the heavy oak door. "You'll see them in the morning."

Fly sprang out of the Land-Rover and bounded up the steps, while his master lifted out Fiona's bags and led the way into the house. The entrance hall was large and lofty, the white walls hung with hunting prints and adorned with foxes' masks. By the door hung a wall rack full of hunting whips and fly whisks made of dyed horse hair. A profusion of doors opened off the hall in every direction, and a wide oak staircase with massive carved bannisters led to the upper regions, whence came the sound of girls' voices.

"Come into the drawing room and meet Mrs. Anstruther," said her guide, opening the first door on the right. "She'll show you to your room and introduce you to the others."

Mrs. Anstruther was sitting in a chair by the fire, surrounded by three blue-brindled whippets. She put down the book she was reading and rose to her feet. Fiona observed that this tall, elegant woman in the turquoise house-coat was as different from Miss Dodd as it was possible for anyone to be.

"So this is Fiona!" she said, as she advanced with her hand outstretched. "Welcome to Wellesley Hall, and I hope you'll be very happy here." Her cool grey eyes looked smilingly into Fiona's own.

"I'm sure I shall," murmured Fiona, taking in every detail of the gracious room with its parquet floor, its pale Chinese carpet, the subdued pastel damask of its curtains and covers. Over the Adam mantlepiece, whose marble shelf was adorned with Dresden figures, hung a portrait of an exceedingly good-looking young man in Army uniform. He bore a strong resemblance to the Colonel, yet he had his mother's height and slim build and her enormous grey eyes.

Mrs. Anstruther, following her gaze, announced: "That's Gavin, our son. You'll meet him presently—he helps us here and is in charge of the stables. Now, come along and we'll go up to your room, and then I'll take you to the common-room and introduce you to the other girls."

The whippets followed her, after a supercilious inspection of Fiona, and Fiona followed them out of the drawing room and up the staircase, with the Colonel bringing up the rear carrying her suitcases. It was a large, rambling house, and they seemed to walk miles over mushroom-coloured, carpeted landings, before the little procession halted and Mrs. Anstruther opened a white door.

It was a pleasant room, apart from what appeared to Fiona to be rather "busy" wall paper. There were two beds draped with white spreads, two heavy mahogany chests of drawers that also did duty as dressing tables, a couple of comfortable-looking easy chairs covered with pink and green chintz and matching the short curtains which hung round the leaded casement window.

One of the dressing tables was bare, except for its mirror and a linen bureau scarf. The other held toilet articles and several framed photographs.

"We've put you in with Lindsay Fothergill," explained Mrs. Anstruther. "Her father is a Master of Hounds in Wales. I think you'll get along very well. You'll soon find you have plenty in common."

Fiona had never shared a room with anyone before and she found herself hoping devoutly that Mrs. Anstruther was right.

"Now, come along downstairs and meet the others. Dinner will be served in a little while."

Someone turned off the gramophone as they entered the common-room. It was large and well-lit, furnished chiefly with sofas and easy chairs in Jacobean covers, and a set of prints by Snaffles hung on the walls. Some twenty girls got to their feet and turned to inspect the new arrival as she was presented to them. Then an extremely pretty girl with long, ash blonde hair detached herself from the group and came towards them.

"This is Lindsay, your room-mate," announced Mrs. Anstruther.

A pair of piercing blue eyes appraised Fiona, evincing little interest in what they saw. "How do you do," acknowledged their owner briefly.

"Now, Fiona, all of the girls are split into two watches. You have been put on the morning watch, which means that you spend the morning in the stables and the afternoon on your other subjects. Next week you will change over and ride in the afternoon. To-morrow morning the first bell will go at seven, and that means stables at half-past." Just then the dinner bell sounded. "Now, Lindsay will show you to the dining-room and I will see you later on."

There was a general exodus to the dining-room, where two long refectory tables stretched side by side down the centre. As they took their places Fiona found herself sitting at the end between her room-mate and a short, dumpy little Frenchwoman with straight grey hair and steel-rimmed spectacles. Opposite was a large, dark girl with dimples and a friendly smile.

"I'm Elizabeth Colquhoun," she said, by way of introduction. "This is Ma'amselle. We are supposed to talk French at meals but we seldom do because she understands us better in English—don't you, Ma'amselle?"

"*En français, ma petite, s'il vous plaît,*" commanded the little Frenchwoman, ladling steaming soup out on to deep plates which were passed along the table.

In between passing plates, Fiona looked around her. At the top of the room was a small, round table where Colonel and Mrs. Anstruther were sitting with a tall young man in a dark grey suit. Elizabeth volunteered:

"That's the glamorous Gavin with his doting parents. He's inclined to be a little pleased with himself, but he's the most attractive person you'll see around here. Isn't he, Lindsay?" she finished with a knowing look at the fair girl.

Lindsay tossed her head and did not reply to this sally. "Where do you ride?" she asked Fiona in a voice that implied complete disinterest.

"In Rotten Row," replied Fiona, pausing in the attack on her soup. "I live in London and there isn't anywhere else to ride."

"Of course," said Lindsay, too politely. Fiona felt that she had already put up a fearsome array of irredeemable black marks, and that Mrs. Anstruther had been utterly wrong in supposing that she and this supercilious girl were going to get along together. She wished she were rooming with Elizabeth, with whom Lindsay's superior attitude obviously cut no ice, while it made Fiona feel two feet high.

When dinner was over they returned to the common-room. Lindsay rushed to the record player and put on a top-twenty tune, and others started to dance. Fiona stood alone, feeling very new, until suddenly she found Elizabeth by her side.

"Would you like to come and see the stables?" she asked. "They are really supposed to be out of bounds after we're changed for dinner, but I don't expect anyone will mind."

"I'd love to!" exclaimed Fiona, brightening

immediately. She followed her guide out of the house through a side door. It was a warm night of bright moonlight, and the lights from the common-room shone right across the large tree-lined lawn. Moths and larger shapes, which Fiona felt uncomfortably might be bats, hovered about them.

They walked along a stone-flagged path through a gate in the garden wall, and Elizabeth switched on a light in the stable yard. There was a chorus of sleepy whinnies from the long row of loose-boxes opposite, and great rustlings of straw. Fiona gazed entranced as heads began to appear at the open top of each half-door.

"Come on—we'll start at the top and work our way down. This, by the way, is the covered school where we do our school work—dressage, in fact. This pony in the first box is Harkaway. He's a mug's ride in the school but he's tremendous out hunting."

Elizabeth pushed back the latch and opened the door to reveal a bay cob, knee deep in fresh wheat straw, shrouded in a jute night rug. He was too busy pulling at his hay net to pay them much heed, but he turned his long, wise head and a knucker of welcome bubbled in his throat.

"You'll probably ride him to-morrow," remarked Elizabeth. "The new people generally start on him."

Fiona patted the hard, muscular neck and said,

in what she hoped to be a professional tone: "What a wonderful outlook he's got." She was not quite sure what this meant, but Miss Dodd's aged groom said it regularly about the only horse in the stable who was at all comfortable to ride, and she had a vague notion that it referred to a horse's neck and shoulders.

Next door, as they worked their way down the long line of boxes, stood something very different. A thoroughbred chestnut mare came towards them with wildly rolling eyes and bared teeth, her ears laid flat along her neck. Fiona recoiled instinctively and Elizabeth laughed.

"Don't mind her—she's as quiet as a lamb really, but it amuses her to pretend to be a man-eater. She's a wonderful ride, but she's a bit tetchy in her box. She came out of training, and we think some lad knocked her about in a racing stable. Her name is Mistinguett. All right, old girl," and she stroked the nose of the mare, who immediately grew quiet and rubbed her head on Elizabeth's shoulder.

"This one's very special," went on Elizabeth, shutting the box door and turning to the grey Anglo-Arab who was regarding them with great interest. "He is Endymion, and he's Mrs. Anstruther's future dressage horse. He's only five." She opened the door and entered the box, and Fiona followed her. Suddenly the grey horse, seeking adventure, pushed past them, shoved the door wide with his chest and was standing outside in the yard. Elizabeth lunged after him and he trotted towards the garden gate and was lost to their sight.

"Great Scott!" Elizabeth ejaculated softly. "That's done it! He'll play havoc with the lawn. Pray heaven the front gate is shut or he'll be out on the road."

"It was all my fault," said Fiona, aghast. "I should have shut the door."

"Can't be helped—come on, we must try and catch him."

They raced back the way they had come, and there was the grey horse, a ghostly shape on the lawn, standing in the shaft of light that came from an upstairs window. He was grazing, but as soon as he saw them he knew they spelt capture and, kicking up his heels, he tore down to the dark shrubbery at the far end of the garden.

"Quick, Fiona, run and see if the front gate's shut," said Elizabeth. "I'll get him away from the shrubbery—there's a yew tree there and if he eats any of that it'll kill him."

Fiona rushed to do as she was bid and sent up a silent prayer of thanks that Endymion had not got out on to the road and slipped down or run into a car. When she returned, a breathless Elizabeth was trying to corner the horse, but when he found her closing in on him he dashed past her towards the house again.

Even in the semi-dark Fiona could see the holes he was making in the well-kept lawn. Then, to make it worse, a horse called from the stables, and another answered. Next, Endymion took up the refrain, and a head appeared at the open upstairs window.

"What the . . .!" said a man's voice. "What's going on down there?"

"We've let Endymion out, and we can't lay a hand on him," called Elizabeth. "Do please come and help us, Gavin."

The head disappeared, and presently its angry owner appeared. He glanced briefly at Fiona, took from Elizabeth the head-collar she had snatched from Endymion's box and assumed command. The young horse meanwhile stopped his grazing and stared warily at them.

"Now, you two stay here and I'll try to catch him first," said Gavin. "If I can't we'll get him into a corner and one of you can go for a bowl of corn."

But Endymion knew when the game was up. He stood as though butter wouldn't melt in his mouth while Gavin walked up to him, slipped the head-collar rope around his neck and pulled the noseband up over his muzzle. Then he allowed himself to be led away to his box, while his would-be captors followed disconsolately behind.

"Now, what on earth were you doing?" asked Gavin sternly when he slid the door latch home.

"Well, I was showing Fiona the horses—she only arrived this evening . . ." "And I forgot to shut the door," finished Fiona. "It was all my fault, and I'm awfully sorry."

"So you should be, too," snapped the young man, his eyes blazing. "It's not a very good beginning, is it? That's a valuable horse and it's a miracle that he didn't hurt himself. The lawn's in a heck of a state and there'll be trouble when my parents see it. You'd better cut along in and I'll break the news. And next time, keep out of the stables, unless there's somebody responsible around."

"I'm most awfully sorry, Elizabeth," said Fiona miserably as they went back to the house. "He was furious, wasn't he?"

"Oh, he'll get over it," said Elizabeth philosophically. "Don't worry—that sort of thing could happen to anyone. Bad luck, though, on your first night here. He didn't need to be quite so rude."

"Well, where have you two been?" asked Lindsay as they went back into the common-room.

Elizabeth shot Fiona a warning glance. "Oh, just to look at the horses," she replied airily. "You should have been with us—Gavin's out there now.

Lindsay flushed and turned away.

"Don't tell her a thing," Elizabeth warned

Fiona in a low voice. "She'll find out soon enough, I don't doubt, but it's no concern of hers. Well, I'm for bed, how about you?"

"Me too—I've got all my unpacking to do yet."

"*And* stable duty at the crack of dawn to-morrow!" laughed Elizabeth. "I hope Master Gavin's in a better mood by then, but the early morning isn't really his best time!"

CHAPTER III

First Morning

The stable bell, melodious but none the less insistent, awakened Fiona the following morning. She opened her eyes to find the early morning sunshine streaming into the strange room. Lindsay stirred beneath her blankets, and Fiona sprang out of bed and hurried off with her sponge-bag to the bathroom to avoid the queue that she guessed would form there shortly.

When she returned Lindsay opened her eyes reluctantly, yawned, stretched and rolled over in bed. They exchanged "good mornings" and Fiona began to pull on the jodhpurs, shirt and sweater that she had left ready the night before.

Idly, Lindsay contemplated her room-mate's hasty dressing. Under her steady stare Fiona, who had been until now extremely proud of her riding clothes, began to wonder if there were not something terribly wrong with them. Nor was she left long in doubt.

"*Where* did you get those jodhpurs?" Lindsay asked at last.

"In London," she replied in some surprise.

"Who made them?" Lindsay's tone implied serious doubts as to whether they had been made at all. She got slowly out of bed and was soon thrusting her own elegant legs into a well-worn pair of hand-sewn jodhpurs, so beautifully cut that she appeared to have been poured into them. Fiona gazed in admiration.

"Who made those?" she asked.

"A little tailor in Ledbury who makes for my father and the hunt staff. He knows his job," Lindsay said briefly. Fiona, glancing down at the mass of wrinkles which enveloped her from knee to ankle, silently conceded the point. She noted, too, Lindsay's soberly striped regimental-type tie and felt a sudden distaste for the disembodied horses which peered inanely from her own.

There was a knock on the door and Elizabeth burst in.

"Come on, you two. Only five minutes left, and Gavin will be on the warpath if we're late."

Lindsay went on combing her hair—a seemingly interminable operation. "You and Fiona go ahead, I shan't be long."

"Don't worry about last night," remarked Elizabeth reassuringly as they went downstairs. "Mrs. Anstruther has forgiven us because you're a new arrival and you start the day with a clean slate."

The stable yard was already a hive of activity Gavin, in his shirt-sleeves and jeans, was directing operations.

"'Morning," he greeted them cheerfully. "Fiona, you're to do Harkaway this week. Elizabeth will show you how we do things here, as it's your first morning. Oh, and by the way, don't leave any doors open this time!" He grinned and Fiona smiled shamefacedly back at him.

Harkaway had been innured against being "done" by strangers after a succession of pupils of very varying degrees of experience or ineptitude. He put up with Fiona's ministrations with a good grace once his manger was full of the corn, bran and chaff mixture which she and Elizabeth prepared in the feed store.

For the next half-hour, Fiona was occupied in mucking out the loose box, piling up the clean straw at the back and carting the manure away in a wheelbarrow: throwing back the cob's rug and "quartering" him, or grooming him superficially to prepare him for morning exercise: and filling his bucket and hay net.

The routine was far more thorough than that which had prevailed in Miss Dodd's somewhat slapdash establishment, and Fiona had barely completed her tasks when the breakfast bell rang.

At the table Fiona found herself sitting next to the assistant riding instructress, Deidre, whom she had already seen at morning stables. Deidre lived at home on her parents' farm a couple of miles away, but she arrived at Wellesley Hall in the early morning and remained there all day. She was a large, good-natured, rather plain young woman in her twenties with a businesslike manner and a quite remarkable lack of charm, redeemed by a considerable sense of humour and a rough kindliness which she distributed indiscriminately both to humans and to horses.

Fiona, whose breakfast usually consisted of fruit and coffee, found herself consuming a liberal amount of porridge, bacon and eggs and toast and marmalade. After they had made their beds they reported back to the stables for their ride.

"The morning ride has to work in the school," Elizabeth explained. "Next week, when we ride in the afternoon, we go out across country with Gavin but this week we have a steady diet of Deidre's dressage."

Fiona collected Harkaway's saddle and bridle from the old-fashioned tack room with its shining array of bits in glass cupboards and its satisfying smell of well-tended leather. Then she saddled up the cob and led him out of his box. As he emerged into the yard where half a dozen riders were already mounted he pricked his ears and looked around him. Fiona gathered up the reins and mounted neatly while Deidre, seated upon the young dressage horse, smiled her approval.

They lined up and rode off into the school in single file. Elizabeth was riding a big, chestnut heavy-weight hunter with a plainish head, and Lindsay was on a big, raking, brown ex-steeplechaser which Fiona knew she had brought with her from Wales.

Harkaway lost interest immediately when he found that they were staying in the school instead of going out into the country. As Fiona rode him through the big double doors she felt the fire and enthusiasm leaving him abruptly, and he went round on the tan like one of Miss Dodd's patent safeties carrying its third client of the day around the Row. Fiona squeezed him up into his bridle with her legs, but his response was only half-hearted. Clearly this was not his idea of an amusing morning.

As they circled the wooden walls of the school Deidre took up her stand in the centre. "To-day," she announced, "we are going to concentrate first on the extended paces. These horses are all half asleep and they need waking up. I want you to shorten your reins and prepare to trot. Use your legs and your seat bones to push your horses on."

Harkaway, who was bringing up the rear of the ride, was not prepared to exert himself any more than was strictly necessary, but Fiona hoped that she was not doing too badly. So far, at least, she had escaped being called out for a misdemeanour.

So, too, had Elizabeth, but some of the others, Lindsay among them, had incurred Deidre's disapproval. Her homilies, delivered in broad Gloucestershire, were pithy and to the point.

"Can't you control that ruddy racehorse?" she demanded scornfully as Lindsay's animal fly-bucked round a corner. "Lunatic animal seems to think he's going down to the start at Cheltenham."

Harkaway's version of an extended trot was acutely uncomfortable, and Fiona was beginning to grit her teeth when Deidre finally decided to call a halt and switch to work on two tracks. First she gave a demonstration of how it should be done, and as they lined up to watch her crablike progress down the length of the school Fiona found herself between a sulky Lindsay, muttering in low tones about the absurdity and general uselessness of dressage, and a small, cheery-looking girl with close-cropped dark hair. Her name was Caroline and she was apparently quite unmoved by the fact that she and the thoroughbred chestnut mare she was riding were unable to do anything right. Even now the mare was moving restlessly about, tossing her head and taking surreptitious nips at her neighbours.

Harkaway's ears went back and his expression grew more and more sour. At last, tried beyond all endurance, he reached over and closed his teeth upon the neck of his tormentor, who let out an anguished squeal.

Fiona, who was already somewhat concerned at the prospect of being asked to execute a movement on two tracks—a refinement which was not included in Miss Dodd's curriculum—was covered with confusion. Lindsay threw her a scornful look and Deidre summed up the situation with a glance. Caroline the chief transgressor, grimaced wryly.

"Don't crowd one another or someone is going to get kicked," ordered Deidre. "Caroline, keep that biting brute away from the others. You can come out and show us how work on two tracks should be done."

They rounded off the lesson with jumping a couple of low poles that were placed on wings in the centre of the school. Fiona felt that she had acquitted herself reasonably well so far but this, she knew, would prove to be her Waterloo. Hyde Park did not boast a single jumpable fence and Fiona had never ridden a horse over one in her life.

Thankful that her turn came last, she watched the others minutely as, one by one, they cantered up to the small parallels and landed on the other side. Though no one actually fell off, by no means everybody covered herself with glory. Elizabeth got "left behind" and jabbed her horse badly in the mouth, which, judging by Deidre's caustic comments, appeared to be the cardinal sin. Lindsay and her steeplechaser skimmed over the obstacle like a bird, however, and even Caroline and her fidgety chestnut contrived to jump it quite professionally.

At last it was Harkaway's turn, and Fiona set off with a pounding heart, her teeth clenched tightly, offering up a silent prayer that she might keep the cob between herself and the floor of the riding school. Recalling Elizabeth's misadventure she took care to position herself well-forward in the saddle, and she rose in her stirrup irons as they took off.

In point of fact, she need not have worried. Harkaway knew his job, and he loved jumping. They were up and over and had landed safely on the other side before Fiona had time to realise anything except the fact that it was the most glorious sensation she had ever experienced.

But her triumph was, after all, to be short-lived. hile she was still sitting well-forward with her hands up Harkaway's neck he put his head down and gave a joyful little buck. Fiona fell lightly on to the soft tan of the riding school floor, physically quite unhurt but feeling every kind of a fool.

"Bad luck," said Deidre kindly. "But that should never have happened, you know. Get back into the saddle as soon as your horse touches down, and keep hold of his head. He's feeling a bit above himself this morning after his Sunday rest, and you did put temptation in his way."

A crimson Fiona remounted and looked almost involuntarily across at Lindsay. A smile was playing around her room-mate's lips, and Fiona vowed then and there that she would eventually ride better than her rival.

The lesson was over, but as the others filed back to the stable yard Deidre kept Fiona behind. "Have you ever jumped a fence before?" she asked.

Fiona shook her head.

"Silly, you should have said so. You did very well, but that was too big a fence for a complete beginner. I'll give you a few lessons on your own and you'll soon catch up with the others. Most of them have been hunting and jumping for years, you know. Now, off you go and unsaddle Harkaway. And don't worry about falling off. We've all done it, many times, and no one thinks anything of it."

Fiona flashed her a grateful smile and they rode out of the school together. Elizabeth grinned as she passed on her way to the tack room with her horse's saddle and bridle in her arms.

"Hurry up!" she called. "When we've strapped the horses and watered and fed them we have a French session with Mam'selle."

After lunch came an hour of needlework, and

then they repaired to the kitchen for a domestic-science lesson.

"This place is a racket!" Elizabeth confided laughingly to Fiona as they stood side by side making pastry. "Needlework consists for the most part of darning the Colonel's and Gavin's socks and repairing their shirts, and domestic science is whipping up little delicacies for their dinner. We only get them if they go wrong. Ah well, nothing lasts forever, I suppose!"

They made enough chicken vol-au-vents for the entire household, however, and then it was tea-time. The others, who had cooked and sewn in the morning and now came in with flushed cheeks from their cross-country ride, joined them as they sat around in the common-room, for tea was an informal meal.

"What comes next?" asked Fiona, as she did full justice to a buttered crumpet.

"We actually have an hour to ourselves," Elizabeth told her. "Dinner's at seven, though, and we have to get out of our jodhpurs and re-appear looking like ladies. Afterwards there's a horribly hearty session of country dancing before we go to bed. Then we come to the end of a perfect day—more dead than alive!"

After tea Fiona wandered into the garden by herself. It was a glorious late September evening. The sun, though by now it had lost its strength, still shone on the stone walls and the fields, and the trees cast huge shadows on the grass. The peace was broken only by bird song until, quite suddenly, there was a thunder of galloping hoofs from the field at the front of the house.

The young horses were staging a mock race. With manes flying and tails streaming straight out behind them they careered over to the wooden fence, kicking and biting playfully at one another as they came. Then they stopped dead in their flight and stood with their pink-lined nostrils dilated, breathing heavily, their flanks heaving with their recent exertions.

Fiona crossed the drive and went towards them, wishing that she had some sugar in her pocket. She gazed admiringly at the bay Irish colt, the problem horse, and he looked back at her with interest. His eyes were proud, she thought, but kindly. He did not look a rogue. "If only," thought Fiona, "I might be able to break him—if I knew enough. I'd give a lot to be able to ride him!"

She reached out a hand, and the colt surprised her by stretching forward his soft nose for her caress. She stroked his muzzle softly. It felt like velvet beneath her fingers. Then two more inquisitive noses nuzzled at her as the other colts felt that they might be missing something. But the bay horse turned and nipped each of them in turn, and they retreated with indignant squeals, leaving Fiona's favourite in full possession of the field.

"Do you like young horses?" inquired a voice behind her.

Fiona, who had been so engrossed that she had not heard Gavin's footsteps on the gravel, spun around quickly, startled by the sound of his voice. He smiled and came to lean on the fence beside her.

"I've never really known any, but I do like this one awfully. I'd love to ride him one day."

"So would I!" admitted Gavin ruefully. "Unfortunately we haven't been able to make much progress with him so far. He's been a devil since he came here, and he's not really broken yet. I can't get to the bottom of him at all, but we'll have to get started on him again soon. He's done nothing at all since the spring, when we fought a losing battle with him. Would you like to help me when I tackle him again?"

"Why—I'd love to, more than anything," exclaimed Fiona in a rush. "The only thing is, I don't know that I'd be much help to you. I've only ever ridden made horses."

"Never mind—you'll learn," said Gavin comfortingly. "It's a nice change to find someone who doesn't pretend to know it all."

"What do you call him?" asked Fiona.

"He hasn't been given a name so far. What do you think would suit him?"

Fiona thought for a moment and then, recalling

a rogue horse in a book that she had read, said: "How about Lucifer?"

Gavin considered the suggestion and then nodded his assent. "Lucifer he is. I like it. Well, in a few weeks you and I will start on him. Maybe this time we'll make a job of it and then he can start to earn his keep instead of eating his head off out here."

They walked back to the house together. Fly, the old lurcher, was lying in the sun at the top of the steps, looking contemptuously at his mistress's lively whippets who were chasing each other flat out around the lawn. As they went through the front door Fiona heard her name being called from the drawing room.

"That's Mother," said Gavin. "Go and have a word with her. See you later."

Mrs. Anstruther, wearing a brown, herringbone riding coat and a pair of very light fawn jodhpurs, superior even to Lindsay's in cut, was arranging flowers in a white boat-shaped vase.

"Well, Fiona," she said with a smile, "how are you settling down? Are you beginning to feel at home here?"

"Oh yes, thank you. But I'm awfully sorry I let your horse out last night."

"Never mind. That's finished with, and no harm was done. I know you won't make that mistake again. Deidre tells me that you ride quite nicely, though you haven't done much jumping. She's going to give you some special jumping lessons and then you can go hunting with the others. How did you like Harkaway?"

"He's terrific!" declared Fiona enthusiastically. "I came off him this morning but it was entirely my fault."

"He'll take good care of you out hunting and give you a lot of fun. Well, I'm glad you are happy here with us. Don't forget, if anything is bothering you at any time you must come and see me and we'll put it right."

Fiona nodded.

"Now I mustn't keep you here talking any longer, or you'll be late for dinner."

When Fiona got up to her bedroom she found that Lindsay had already bathed and was sitting in front of a mirror in her dressing gown, brushing her hair again.

"At last!" she greeted her. "You'd better hurry, there's only about twenty minutes left until dinner time. I see you've been having a cosy time with Gavin," she finished casually—a shade too casually, Fiona surmised.

"Oh, he came along when I was looking at the young horses."

"He was livid about your letting his mother's horse out last night," went on Lindsay, conversationally. "I only heard about it this morning. Was he very unpleasant about it just now? I saw you with him out of the bathroom window!"

"Not at all," Fiona replied, detecting a hopeful note in Lindsay's voice. She could not resist adding: "He says I can help him to break the bay colt in a few weeks' time."

The other girl looked furious but said nothing further. Fiona went and had her bath, and when she came back to the bedroom Lindsay had gone downstairs.

CHAPTER IV

Hunting

UNDER DEIDRE's tutelage Fiona soon became capable of putting up quite a good performance over small fences, and eventually the day arrived when she was pronounced fit to go hunting. Gavin even volunteered to keep an eye on her the following morning, and Lindsay, somewhat to her surprise, gave her what amounted to a pre-hunting lecture in bed that night.

The two girls had jogged along fairly well together recently, though there was still a slight uneasiness about their relationship. Fiona had at least the satisfaction of knowing that she was becoming daily more proficient and experienced, both in the stables and on a horse. She had been promoted to riding several different horses in the school, though she was being relegated to Harkaway again for her first day's hunting.

"If I were you, I'd stay near the back and follow the others," Lindsay advised her. "That way you can't do very much damage. The cardinal sins out hunting are to head the fox and to kick a hound, and you are unlikely to do either at the tail of the field. You won't have to jump enormous places, either, because someone is sure to have broken them down before you."

Fiona was so excited the following morning that she felt slightly sick, and she had the greatest difficulty in eating her breakfast. She was never, at the best of times, unduly endowed with self-confidence, and now she was terrified that she would disgrace herself and annoy Gavin, who had so kindly offered to look after her. Her clothes were another sore point. Although she had cleaned her jodhpur boots until they shone like antique furniture, and brushed her coat, cap and jodhpurs until they were innocent of a single stray horse hair or a speck of dust, she was acutely conscious of the fact that while she was going hunting in jodhpurs and a tweed coat, almost everyone else, Lindsay and Elizabeth included, had turned out in black coats, breeches and long, black hunting boots. The fact that she could now, with impunity, use for the first time the stag-horn handled hunting whip which had adorned for so many years the wall above the mantlepiece of her bedroom at home, afforded her small consolation.

Once mounted, however, with a packet of sandwiches in her pocket, she forgot all about her worries and tribulations in the excitement of the moment. Harkaway knew full well that to-day was a hunting day, and he was on his toes and as keen as mustard. Winter comes early in the

Cotswolds, and it was a glorious November morning of brilliant sunshine, with just the right amount of nip in the air. The horses had all been clipped out for the opening meet the week before, and Harkaway's coat looked like a sea-lion that Fiona had once seen asleep in its cage at a circus.

Every available horse went out from Wellesley Hall that morning. Mrs. Anstruther, beautifully turned out in a blue habit, a silk hat and a veil, was riding a grey dressage horse side-saddle. Gavin and his father, in toppers and red coats, were riding two of the young horses that they later hoped to sell. Some twelve of the girls were hunting too, and it was a sizeable contingent that made its way out of the stable yard under the old stone archway and wound along the drive towards the main road.

The colts in the field created quite a diversion when they saw them. They tore up and down, whinnying wildly, and the ridden horses reacted with varying amounts of enthusiasm. The older horses strode on superciliously without a glance at these ill-mannered youngsters, but both Gavin's and the Colonel's horses arched their necks and pranced along, blowing vigorously down their noses, while Mrs. Anstruthers' dressage horse humped his back and did his best to buck. Even Harkaway played with his bit and started to jog, defying all Fiona's efforts to get him back into a walk.

Truth to tell, the cob, through Fiona did not know it, was not best pleased at being kept at the back. He was bringing up the rear of the procession alongside Elizabeth on her chestnut heavyweight, one of the few animals present who remained quite unmoved by the excitement. Indeed, he looked as though he would not so much as twitch an eyelid were a bomb to explode beside him.

On the main road they very soon met a double-decker bus, but the driver slowed down considerately until the cavalcade had passed. Just before they turned off down a side road that led to the village where the meet was to be held they met an ambulance, coming towards them at a considerable rate. As it roared past them, Gavin's horse shied and nearly landed in the ditch.

"Idiot!" commented Elizabeth. "It's funny how ambulances always seem to drive past horses full tilt. They must be trying to drum up a bit of trade!"

Fiona had read enough hunting books to be pretty well prepared for what was going to happen, but they did not prepare her for the thrill she was to feel as they clattered up the road between ancient stone cottages, each with its women and children at the gate, and came upon the hounds, the Master and the hunt servants outside the village pub. Her heart leapt up into her throat at the sight of them, and she could scarcely, even now, believe that she was a part, however small and unimportant, of the splendid pageant.

Gavin and his father doffed their hats and said good-morning to the Master, and then the landlord of the public house appeared with a tray of drinks, Fiona followed Elizabeth's lead and refused a stirrup cup when she was offered it, though she had always longed to taste cherry brandy. She knew, however, that she must keep her wits about her, to-day of all days, and for all she knew the dark red liqueur in the tiny glasses might have all sorts of unforseen effects.

Lindsay, however, had no such qualms. When Fiona saw her disappearing behind a horse-box to swallow what was undoubtedly her third glass of cherry brandy she turned back to Elizabeth.

"Won't she get drunk?" she asked.

"Not she. Her father drinks like a fish and Lindsay can knock them back, all right, without batting an eyelid. She'd better not let Mrs. Anstruther see her, though. Of course, she's too clever for that, but she's been warned about this sort of thing out hunting before. If she gets caught to-day she'll be sent home."

Riders were still arriving from all directions, for this was a popular meet over first-class hunting country, and always attracted a big field. Young riders were in the minority, for this was term-time, but Fiona noticed many men in red coats and silk hats and almost as many farmers wearing black coats and bowler hats. There were several elegant ladies riding side-saddle, and any number of younger women in hunting caps riding astride. Every one seemed to know everyone else, and friendly greetings and a good deal of cheery badinage were exchanged as the crowd which thronged the roadway outside the inn grew bigger and bigger.

Presently the huntsman blew his horn. His beautiful hounds, who had been milling impatiently around him, eager to get on with their job, set out behind him to draw the first covert, followed by the two whippers-in. Then came the Master, the Field Master, and a man who had been collecting money in his cap and must, Fiona knew, be the Hunt Secretary. They were almost out of sight before Fiona, obeying Lindsay's instructions meticulously and keeping Harkaway right at the back, set off down the road after the main body of the hunt.

Alongside her rode a very old lady riding an equally ancient grey cob under a side-saddle. She smiled at Fiona and said: "Don't I recognise Harkaway? You must be one of the young ladies from Wellesley Hall."

Fiona introduced herself and said that it was her first day's hunting.

"I hope you enjoy it. Harkaway's a wonderful hunter," remarked her companion. "He and Nimrod, my cob, are very old friends. Neither of them is as young as he might be, but they never allow themselves to get left."

Fiona was actually not enjoying herself as much as she had hoped, for Harkaway was proving a double-handful to hold. He kept tossing his head and trying to edge up and pass the other horses. Just ahead was a fidgety-looking brown thoroughbred mare with a red ribbon affixed to her tail. Fiona knew that this was the hall-mark of a kicker, and she was having her work cut out to prevent Harkaway, who seemed to be bent on self-destruction, going up too close. The grey cob was likewise setting his jaw and doing his best to forge ahead.

"Exhausting, aren't they?" laughed the old lady, who seemed to be quite unperturbed by the prospect of having her arms pulled out of their sockets. "Thank goodness they're going to draw the big wood up there on the right. These two will soon settle down when hounds start to run and they get a chance to stretch their legs."

Fiona hoped devoutly that this might be so. They arrived at the covert at last and filed through the gateway to spread out on one side of the wood. Hounds had disappeared, but she could hear them crashing through the undergrowth encouraged by their huntsman's thrilling cries. Occasionally a hound whimpered uncertainly, and the sound was followed by: "Huic to Dexter! Huic, huic!"

At last a much more determined yelping, shrill and high-pitched, came from the other end of the wood, where Fiona could see Gavin and his father waiting expectantly for the fox to break covert. She heard galloping hoofs as the huntsman hurried to the scene, blowing short blasts on his horn to bring the rest of the pack with him. Presently another hound spoke, then several more gave tongue. The field shortened their reins, horses tensed and peered deep into the wood.

"They sound like business now," observed a man near Fiona, throwing away his cigarette. "It shouldn't be long before we have a hunt."

Harkaway stood like a rock while a small red shadow flitted out between the trees quite close to where they were standing and loped off, apparently quite unconcerned and in no especial hurry, across the field. Fiona sat transfixed, but the man who had just spoken raised his hat high in the air and halloaed the fox away. With the greatest difficulty, Fiona managed to control an irresistable impulse to gallop after the fox. She knew that the field must wait until hounds were well away before they themselves made a move to follow.

A stream of black and white and tan came surging out of the wood in full cry, noses to the ground and sterns waving behind them. The huntsman followed them over a low post-and-rails, and then came the whippers-in. They cantered across the field, jumped a thick hedge and disappeared from sight. Now, at last, the field was able to follow. Hats were rammed on and the riders set off in close pursuit. Gavin was in the first flight, and Fiona, obediently restraining Harkaway, saw him glancing round uncertainly over his shoulder. Then the cob started to fly-jump impatiently, and as he fought for his head Fiona forgot everything else but the supreme importance of controlling him and remaining out of the way.

When she decided that it was safe to let him go he thundered away across the field after the others as hard as he could go, and Fiona knew that she was very nearly out of control. He passed several horses whose riders had decided to take things easily so early in the day and arrived at the hedge in front of them. Grimly determined to keep her place Fiona just managed to pull him up before he jumped it and make him wait his turn. But Harkaway, whose only thought was to be with hounds, could not understand why he was being thus thwarted. He half-reared in his excitement, and Fiona decided that she would have to let him jump if she were to remain on his back.

She managed to slow him down across the next field, which sloped uphill towards a low stone wall, but then there came a downhill slope and he started pulling hard. When she pulled back at him he set his teeth and started to buck. She was not enjoying herself at all. She tried in vain to get his head up and he bucked again as a couple of horses shot past him. The next moment Fiona was lying on her back in the field and Harkaway was tearing away from her as hard as he could lay legs to the ground.

As she got to her feet a farmer on an unclipped colt pulled up beside her.

"You all right?" he asked.

Fiona nodded miserably.

"Bad luck getting bucked off like that. I've never known Harkaway do that before. I'll go and see if I can catch him for you."

He raised his hat and cantered off, and Fiona, miserable and disgraced, plodded on in the direction which hounds had taken. Nobody passed her now, for she had obeyed her instructions so well that she was right at the end of the hunt. She wondered why she had ever wanted to go hunting at all. She dreaded seeing anyone from Wellesley Hall after having made such an utter fool of herself—and what would Gavin have to say?

She did not have long to wonder. Very soon he appeared on the horizon, riding his own horse and leading a chastened Harkaway who looked now as though he had never thought of bucking in his life. As he drew nearer Fiona could see that Gavin looked annoyed. She realised that she had made him miss the hunt, and felt even more dejected.

"What on earth happened to you?" he greeted her. "I kept looking around for you but you never came, and then I saw Harkaway loose and galloping like mad."

"I tried to keep him at the back, but I simply couldn't hold him."

"Why try and keep him at the back?" demanded Gavin irately. "The whole point of hunting is to be in front. No wonder you got bucked off if you kept pulling Harkaway. He's the best hunter in the world, but he's full of courage and he has to go on. If you'd ridden him on you wouldn't have got into trouble. You aren't frightened to gallop, are you?"

"No. But Lindsay told me that I must keep him behind and stay out of the way, and I did try to. I'm awfully sorry," she finished contritely.

Gavin set his mouth grimly. "Oh, she told you that, did she? I'll have a word with her later. Now, jump up, and you're riding with me for the rest of the day. Hounds have checked a few fields ahead. If we hurry we'll find them and have a hunt yet."

In no time Fiona had remounted and was cantering down to the next stone wall alongside Gavin. Harkaway was going quite differently now, and not even offering to pull. Fiona kept a light feel on his mouth, sat forward and let herself go with him. He rose like a bird at the wall, and Gavin threw her a sideways glance and a grin as they landed together on the other side.

"That's more like it!" he remarked encouragingly. "Feeling better now?"

Fiona nodded. Suddenly she was so confident and happy that she felt like singing. Harkaway was going like a dream, eating up the ground with long, easy strides and jumping the walls like a stag. Hunting *was* glorious, after all!

A couple of fields more and they came suddenly upon the others. The fox had run through a field of sheep and hounds had temporarily lost his scent. But the huntsman left them alone to cast themselves again and almost as soon as Fiona and Gavin arrived they were off once more through a field of kale, hunting with the strong cry that betokened that they were no longer in doubt as to the way their quarry had taken.

"Now, no more hanging back," said Gavin. "We've got a fair start, and we'll see this fox pulled down if we keep going."

The next twenty minutes were sheer poetry. Harkaway and Gavin's young horse, Hotspur, pounded along neck and neck, jumping the walls as they came and soon beginning to leave the rest of the field behind them. Fiona was delighted when they caught up with Lindsay and her steeplechaser. She shot Fiona a glance of amazed annoyance, and when the old 'chaser pecked and nearly fell over a wall Harkaway forged ahead and his rider forgot her rival. There was, in any case, no room in her mind for anything but the job at hand, which was to keep abreast of Gavin and to ride Harkaway as well as she could.

The cob had settled down beautifully now. He was not pulling an ounce, and Fiona at last was finding him a wonderfully easy ride. All she had to do was to sit there and leave him alone, and he did the rest. He was indeed a patent safety, and he took such care of himself that anyone could have riden him.

Now the bare length of a field separated them from the pack ahead, and they were nearly level with the Master and Colonel Anstruther.

"Enjoying yourself?" called Gavin.

Fiona grinned and nodded her head. She was getting a little short of breath by now but she knew that she would be quite contented to go on like this forever. But all good things come to an end. Suddenly Gavin shouted: "By Jove, they're coursing him now!" and she saw the red form of the fox only slightly ahead of hounds. Minutes later, the pack was milling around a drain that ran under the lane ahead, and she knew that their fox had gone to ground.

Gradually more and more people arrived as the hunt staff dismounted from their horses and went to investigate. Fiona and Gavin dismounted too, and she held his horse while he got down on his knees in the ditch.

"Where's Charlie with the terriers?" demanded the Master. "We might bolt him if they come soon. Otherwise we'll leave him for another day. He's given us a good run and saved his brush at the end of it."

Charlie the terrier man, who followed the hunt in the hound van, was nowhere to be seen five minutes later and the huntsman decided to draw again, rather to Fiona's relief. The idea of putting in terriers to force out a tired fox did not appeal to her very greatly, although she knew that hounds deserved a kill.

"I think we'd better give up and make for home," said Gavin regretfully. "That run was quite enough for this youngster, he's only half fit."

They said good-night to the Master and started back along the lane. They were some five miles away from home, and they walked and trotted alternately in order to rest the horses. Both the horses had sweated, but it soon dried to a white powdery substance on their clipped coats.

"I can't understand why Lindsay told you to keep Harkaway at the back," pondered Gavin slowly as they rode along. "Can you?"

Fiona, who had a shrewd suspicion that Lindsay had hoped that she would come to grief, shook her head. "Maybe she didn't realise how keen Harkaway is," she suggested.

"Nonsense," Gavin declared. "She's been here for nearly a year and she's hunted Harkaway herself several times. I think it was a rotten thing to do. Wonder where she is now? I suppose as she's riding her own horse she'll keep him out for another hunt. Useless brute he is, too, in the hunting field. Half of these 'chasers have never been taught to jump. I shouldn't be surprised if he gave her a crashing fall one day."

Later on they caught up with two more of the Wellesley Hall girls, and then a clatter behind them announced Elizabeth's arrival. She was cheery and muddy, and Fiona noticed that she, too, had a suspiciously dirty back. Gavin noticed it too.

"You've bought a bit of ground, I see," he commented. "What happened?"

"This clumsy animal put his foot in a hole, and we both went for six," replied Elizabeth. "I know it's usually my fault, but this time it wasn't."

Gavin grunted and looked sceptical, but he asked no more questions.

When they got back and Fiona led Harkaway into his box he rubbed his sweaty head against her coat and she felt that they now understood one another.

"Poor old fellow, you didn't have much fun at first, did you?" she whispered. "I'll know better, though, the next time."

She put his rugs on and gave him his mash, and then she went in for tea and a bath. Afterwards the girls all came out again to do their horses and clean the tack, and Fiona soon realised that strapping a horse that has been hunting is often very hard work.

When they were busy in the harness room, stripping down the saddles and bridles and sponging off the mud, Gavin put his head around the door. "Hasn't Lindsay got back yet?" he asked. "My mother's beginning to worry about her."

Twilight was already drawing in, and soon it would be dark. No one had seen Lindsay, but just at that moment she rode into the yard. Gavin went over to speak to her.

"She's jolly late," remarked Caroline. "She must have stayed out until hounds went home."

"I think she's got a boy friend," put in Elizabeth. "She was riding in the pocket of that farmer on the young horse all day."

"But I thought she was fond of Gavin?" queried Fiona.

"She is, but she likes to have two or three on a string. Besides, you've rather put her nose out of joint there!"

Fiona flushed and said nothing. On the whole she thought it wiser not to mention the advice that Lindsay had given her about riding Harkaway.

CHAPTER V

Lucifer at School

Towards the end of November Gavin decided to bring the Irish colt, Lucifer, in from the field and begin his education in earnest. Somewhat to Fiona's chagrin, however, some of the other pupils, Lindsay among them, were detailed to assist with the operation. Though she realised that she, with her very limited experience, and Gavin between them were unlikely to succeed with a difficult colt, she had by now come to regard Lucifer as something very nearly akin to her own property. She visited him daily with titbits, and he undoubtedly knew her and looked forward to her visits.

Gavin caught him one evening, and brought him in to the stable yard. The colt was already halter broken, and he showed no resentment at being incarcerated in a loose box.

"No corn for this fellow until he comes to hand a bit," Gavin ordered. "Plenty of hay, and a bran mash now and then, and he'll come to no harm. Nor, which is more to the point, shall we."

"You'll really have to be tough with him this time, for if you fail again we can write him off completely and send him to Stow Fair without a warranty," warned the Colonel.

Lucifer was lunged, and then long-reined, in the school for an hour every morning and afternoon. The gallery was usually full of spectators, too, for everyone was interested to see the progress that was being made with a difficult horse—and progress there undoubtedly was. He was soon walking, trotting, cantering and halting at the word of command, and apart from getting his back up on a cold morning and getting rid of his high spirits with a squeal and a kick he offered no serious resistance to his training. Fiona, once she had mastered some of the art of driving a horse in long reins by dint of practice on some of the made horses, was even entrusted with Lucifer. So far he had not put a foot wrong, and she had begun to believe that all the talk about his being a problem horse was greatly exaggerated.

At length the day came when Gavin pronounced him ready to be backed. They had already accustomed him to being saddled, using first a roller and then a felt pad and finally working up to a saddle. He wore it first in his loose-box, at the same time as he was playing with the keys on a mouthing bit.

"This bit's to encourage him to salivate," Gavin

explained the first time they used it. "A dry mouth is generally a hard one, but a horse that plays with his bit has a good mouth."

They had leaned across the colt's back to accustom him to weight, and they had long-reined him in the school with the saddle flaps first secured, and then flapping loose against his sides. Lucifer remained perfectly unmoved throughout.

"Of course, he's been through all this part before, so it's old history," Gavin told them. "It's when we start to ride him that the fun will start. That's where we came unstuck before."

"I'm not sure that that isn't old history to him too," observed the Colonel, leaning on the door of the loose box and looking in at the bay colt. "We had a horse like that at Weedon just before the war. He was bought unbroken—or so we thought—but in point of fact someone had tried to break him and made a mess of it. We didn't discover it until we tried to ride him. He was a real villain, too. I've had my suspicions about this fellow for some time."

"Did you succeed with the other horse?" asked Fiona anxiously.

"In the end, but it was a long, hard fight. It was worth it, though, because eventually he turned out to be one of the best horses we had. He had a tremendous jump in him and he won a lot of jumping competitions in his time. I won on him myself at Olympia and the Royal Tournament."

"What tactics do you recommend, Father?" asked Gavin.

"I'm afraid it's impossible to lay down any hard and fast rules. You have to treat each case as an individual and treat it as you think best. If the horse is a rogue you may chasten him into becoming a reasonable member of society. If he's simply been mishandled and frightened you will have to be very gentle with him and regain his confidence. Either way it may be just so much waste of time—but he is a lovely horse. He's worth quite a lot of trouble."

"It's unusual to find an Irish horse that's been broken so badly that they've had to admit to a failure," remarked Lindsay. "My father always buys Irish horses for the very reason that no one has ever laid a hand on them."

"That's so, with the ones that run out on the mountains," agreed the Colonel. "But don't forget that horses are bred in the more civilised parts of Ireland too, and there are even 'mugs' in Ireland—and people who don't understand a horse's temperament. Maybe this one was just unlucky."

"Well, I'm going in to throw a leg over him if you'll hold his head, please, Father. Deidre can take the other side—we may need plenty of ballast to stop him becoming airborne. I have vivid recollections of the last time I sat on him!"

Lindsay gave him a leg-up and, talking softly to the colt all the time while Deidre and the Colonel patted his neck soothingly, Gavin was soon sitting in the saddle; Lucifer, Fiona noticed, stood as still as a rock. Only his eyes betrayed him as they rolled suspiciously backwards and forwards.

"So far, so good," remarked the Colonel with satisfaction. "Now, however, comes the proving point. We'll try to get him to move a couple of steps."

He and Deidre pulled gently on each snaffle ring, and Gavin squeezed the colt gently with his legs. Lucifer stood as immovable as the rock of ages. Then Gavin clicked encouragingly and applied more leg pressure. Still there was no response. Finally he tapped the horse with his stick, and suddenly chaos broke loose.

Lucifer plunged forward with a bound, and then he tried to rear. Only the full weight of Deidre and the Colonel restrained him. The colt stood still again for a moment, breathing hard, and then he tried to run backwards.

"Is it vice or fright?" asked Mrs. Anstruther, who had joined them at the box door.

"We'll try kindness first," replied Gavin, stroking the heaving flank beneath him. "I don't want a fight at this stage of the game."

It seemed as though hours had passed, during which time the performance was repeated many times, before they began to feel that they might be winning. Lucifer allowed himself, at last, to take a step forward without trying to turn himself inside out. Gavin patted him and slid off his back.

"This is the time to stop," he said, "While the tide is still with us." He walked around to the horse's head and pulled his ears caressingly. "You silly old fool," he continued softly. "I don't know what you've been through in the past, but I don't intend to hurt you."

Every day the lesson was resumed, and at the end of a week Lucifer allowed himself to be led around his box with Gavin on his back without offering any resistance at all.

"Well, we've accomplished all we can in here," Gavin announced. "The next move is to get him into the school—and if we're due for any more fireworks, I hope we have them there where he'll be easier to control. Though, if he's the horse I think he is, he'll be clever enough to wait until we have him outside in the open before he really turns on the heat."

Gavin turned out to be a pretty reliable prophet. Lucifer was a model of deportment in the school. Indeed, he was almost listless, which Gavin was inclined to interpret as a bad sign.

"He's half-sullen," agreed the Colonel as they discussed their progress one day. "We're due for a battle, you can bank on it, and the sooner it comes the better I'll be pleased. The fitter he becomes, the worse it will be, and this time we simply cannot afford to lose."

Fiona was secretly longing to ride the colt herself, but Gavin allowed no one but himself to sit on his back. Even Deidre, who volunteered one day, was forbidden to mount him.

"I must be there to cope when the trouble starts," Gavin told her. "That is, to try to cope. He may do anything, and we dare not let him get away with it if we can possibly help it."

Then the day arrived when it was decided to ride the colt out of doors. Gavin mounted him in his box and Deidre and the Colonel led him out through the stable yard, across the drive and into a large flat field. Then they let go of the bridle.

"Now you're on your own," said the Colonel. "Be careful—and good luck."

Lucifer set off around the field quietly enough, first at a walk and then at a trot. Then Gavin urged him into a canter. Lucifer hung back reluctantly and Gavin tapped him with his stick—and that was enough. The colt ran backwards, half reared, and then started in to buck. Fiona had never seen a horse buck like it. He twisted and turned like an eel, and seemed determined to turn himself inside out.

"He knows a bit about that job," muttered Deidre. "A green horse doesn't buck like that."

Gavin stuck to him for a remarkable length of time, fighting in vain to get his head up, but at last, after a particularly vicious twist, the bay horse succeeded in putting him down. Then, while Gavin got disconsolately to his feet, he plunged off, snorting, down the field, jumped the wall at the end and disappeared from view.

"He's mad," said the Colonel. "If he gets on to the road he'll be killed for a certainty. I'll get the Land-Rover and go after him—you, Deidre, get a horse and go after him. An animal like that's not worth bothering with. We'll turn him out again and sell him without a character as soon as we can."

"I'm having another go—he's not beating me so easily," said Gavin grimly. "And did you see the way he jumped that wall? He gave it feet to spare—he may be a show jumper yet."

"You're not risking your neck again," ordered his father. "That horse is leaving here as soon as I can arrange it."

He arrived back an hour or so later without having seen a sign of the bay colt. Deidre likewise reappeared empty-handed. Then Gavin went out on a horse, but Lucifer was nowhere to be found.

"He must have got up on to the wolds, unless someone's found him and put him in a field until he's claimed," said the Colonel. "I'd better notify the police, and we'll organise a search party in the morning. It'll be dark in an hour and we won't have a hope of finding him."

That night Fiona could hardly sleep for thinking about Lucifer, lonely and lost and probably frightened too. She could not believe that he was really a rogue. He had only got his back up on the two occasions when Gavin had shown him a stick, which surely indicated that he had been beaten before and was terrified that it might happen again? Perhaps he remembered all sorts of terrible, painful things whenever he felt a stick on his hide.

The following morning she got up early. Her head was aching, and she made her way down to the kitchen to get a cup of tea. There was no one about but the cook, who gave her a cup out of her pot. Just as she was drinking it the telephone rang.

"Whoever can that be at this hour of the morning?" asked cook. "Run and answer it, there's a good girl, while I go on cutting the rinds off this bacon."

Fiona went out into the hall and picked up the receiver. A man's cheery voice greeted her. "Sorry to trouble you so early, but I heard you'd lost a horse and I think I've got him here. At any rate, there was a strange bay colt out in the yard when I went out to the cows, and I've shut him in a box until you can come and see him. Will you tell the Colonel I've called? Roger Murray from Four Ways farm."

Fiona's heart was hammering violently as she hung up the receiver. The germ of an idea was taking root in her mind. She walked very slowly back to the kitchen, and in answer to Cook's inquiry replied that the call had been a wrong number.

"At this time of the day?" exclaimed Cook. "Really, people ought to be more careful!"

Fiona finished her tea quickly and hurried upstairs again. A tremendous plan had formed in her mind. She knew where Four Ways farm was —it was owned by the young man who had been riding the colt on her first day's hunting—and she was determined to go and fetch Lucifer herself, and to ride him home.

Lindsay slept on as Fiona dressed hurriedly, crept downstairs again and bicycled out of the yard. Even now it was barely light, and the country roads were deserted. This, she decided, had both its advantages and its drawbacks. There would be no traffic to frighten the young horse, but equally there would be no one to pick up the pieces if the worst happened and he succeeded in putting her down.

At first she had been startled by her own temerity in assuming that she might succeed where Gavin, with all his experience of breaking young horses, had failed. But soon she was able to convince herself that there was just a vague possibility that this might happen. After all, she probably knew Lucifer better than anyone else, for she had visited him daily for weeks. Her visits to him, moreover, would have pleasant associations in his mind, for her pockets were never empty and she had always treated him kindly. He might, too, be a horse which a girl could manage more easily than a man can, particularly if he had ever received, as seemed likely, harsh treatment at the hands of a man.

In this connection there was, too, the fact that she had noticed one especial point about both of Lucifer's lapses. On each occasion they had been sparked off by the fact of Gavin's touching him with a stick. She reasoned that without a stick, and substituting gentle but firm persuasion, she might avoid a repetition of the previous afternoon's performance. And finally she had this feeling of kinship between herself and the young horse. It had welled up in her when she first set eyes on him the day she arrived at Wellesley Hall, and it had persisted ever since. Some sort of intuition—or was it just optimism?—told her that they were destined to form a partnership.

When she arrived in the Four Ways yard she saw Lucifer's head looking out of a box, and her confidence increased by leaps and bounds when he whinnied a welcome to her. At the sound, Roger Murray emerged from the milking parlour.

"Good morning—well, it's you, is it?" he greeted her. "I thought Mr. Gavin would come. He's a new horse, isn't he? I don't recall seeing him before—what a sort he is!"

"He's just been broken," Fiona told him. "He—er—got away last night. Are his saddle and bridle intact?"

"Quite. I took them off when I put him away, so I'll come and help you saddle him up again. A bit nervous, isn't he?"

"A bit," Fiona agreed.

Lucifer whinnied again and rubbed his head against her when she entered the box.

"Well, he seems to know you, all right!" said the young man cheerfully. "He'll be glad enough to get home, I dare say."

Fiona was overcome with nervousness as she led the horse out into the yard, but she managed to conceal her feelings from the farmer. Lucifer looked enormous as she stood beside him and gathered up the reins. Roger threw her up and she suddenly felt better once she was in the saddle. This was going to be all right, after all.

"Thanks for everything," she said, and clicked to Lucifer. He strode quietly enough towards the gate. "I'll come back for the bicycle later."

"It'll be here!" the farmer promised with a smile, and turned back again towards the milking parlour.

Now she was really on her own. Out on the road she noticed a newly ploughed field, and she wondered whether she ought to give Lucifer a bit of work in the heavy going before venturing any further. In Ireland, she knew, they swore by heavy ploughland to cool the ardour of a horse that was above himself—and it made soft falling, too, if things went wrong. In the end, however, she decided against it. Lucifer was probably tired enough, and hungry too, after wandering about all night. Besides, he was going quite beautifully. Even the listless demeanour that had worried Gavin and his father had quite disappeared. He seemed full of *joie de vivre*, yet at the same time perfectly mannerly.

He was certainly a beautiful ride! After a few minutes experience of his walk Fiona, who had heard that a good walker is a good horse, was longing to try his other paces. She decided to take him home across country—he was not, after all, accustomed to traffic and there was always the possibility of meeting a milk lorry—and she turned off the road and into a copse. Once on the leaf-covered ride between tall beech trees she could resist it no longer, and she asked him to trot. He responded magnificently, and swung along with long, free strides which sent his rider into transports of delight.

At the end of the ride a gate led into a grass field. Lucifer was not of much assistance when it came to opening the gate, but they opened and went through it somehow. Once on the grass Fiona succumbed to an irresistable temptation to have a canter, and soon they were swinging along on the turf. He had the most comfortable canter that Fiona had ever known and she was able to sit right down in the saddle without any of the bumping about that was inevitable on Harkaway.

As they approached the open gate by the hayrick at the far end of the field Fiona threw her last remaining shreds of discretion to the winds and leant forwards, stood up in her irons and closed her legs. Lucifer galloped like the wind. She took a pull as they drew level with the hayrick, and immediately thanked her stars that she had, for a sheep dog rushed out from behind it, barking hysterically. Lucifer shied violently sideways and Fiona spoke to him soothingly and stroked his shoulder. Thank heaven, she thought, she had not fallen off.

They completed their journey more soberly, with just an occasional trot, and walked the last part up the drive to Wellesley Hall. Evidently the sound of the horse's hoofs on the gravel was heard within the house, for Mrs. Anstruther's startled face appeared at the drawing-room window, and when she rode into the stable yard Gavin was emerging from the back door to greet her.

"What on *earth* are you doing?" he demanded, half-annoyed and half in surprise. "Where did you find Lucifer—and why are you riding him? Get off him at once—he might kill you."

Colonel and Mrs. Anstruther came out as Fiona, slipping off Lucifer's back, explained everything that had happened.

"But why didn't you come and tell us? It was very wrong, you know, to take a telephone message that was intended for us, and to act upon it as you thought fit," said Mrs. Anstruther.

"I'm sorry—but somehow I *knew* I could ride him, if I had the chance, and I couldn't bear to think that he was going to be sold and knocked about again. You won't sell him now, will you?"

The Colonel smiled. "Put him away in his box, and we'll see. We shan't send him away this morning, anyway!"

On the whole, much to Fiona's relief, they took it very well. There was no retribution, and Gavin was generous enough not to mind that she had been able to ride a horse that he could not.

"Fiona's come on tremendously since she's been here," he told his parents. "Remember her first day's hunting? I think she'll be good one of these days."

"That is certainly an incredible horse," remarked the Colonel. "A woman's horse, I suppose. There are such things, though you don't find them very often. Of course, it may just have been luck that he didn't play up with Fiona. I suppose we may as well let her go on riding him, but we'll have to watch him very carefully. At the first sign of trouble he'll have to go."

The news about Fiona's escapade soon got about, and she become something of a heroine overnight. Only Lindsay reserved her praise. The two girls lived together only on sufferance, and their conversation was confined strictly to formalities. Fiona had an uncomfortable feeling that her room-mate would reveal herself as an active opponent if the opportunity arose.

CHAPTER VI

South Leach Show

The Christmas holidays came and went. Fiona's parents were relieved, and not a little surprised, to find that their daughter, although she was as horse-minded as ever, had begun to take an interest in her appearance. Even more remarkable, she could produce an edible meal and take care of her clothes, and she was capable of carrying on a conversation, albeit rather a halting one, in quite passable elementary French. No longer did they doubt their wisdom in sending her to Wellesley Hall.

More from a sense of loyalty than because she really wanted to, Fiona went around to see Miss Dodd at the stables in Pelham Place. She found them most depressing. The horses looked older and less sound than she remembered them to be, while their owner seemed untidier than ever. She had become a sort of object lesson to Fiona, who realised now that it was quite unnecessary to look like a horse just because one's life was intimately concerned with them.

Greatly to her relief, she found that the stable

was heavily booked up for the holiday season, and it was therefore impossible for her to ride in the Row, which she now had no desire to do. After her one duty visit she studiously avoided the mews and its occupants, including the bevy of horse-mad girls of whom she had so recently been one.

She took herself off to a reputable tailor and spent her Christmas money on a pair of made-to-measure breeches and jodhpurs. Then she found quite a presentable pair of ready-made hunting boots at a sporting outfitters, and prevailed upon her brother Miles to lend her the money for them. Her riding coat would have to last another season, but at least she would return to Gloucestershire under no sartorial disadvantage. Next winter she made up her mind to invest in a dark-blue hunting coat.

Gavin had been riding Lucifer in the school while she was away, and had experienced no difficulty with him whatsoever. The horse was obviously well on the way to regaining his confidence.

"I took your advice and never carried a stick on him," Gavin told her. "Nor did I venture out. I'm longing to have a hunt on him, though. Gosh, what a ride he is! We'll have to start him jumping soon. Would you like to take it on?"

Fiona accepted with alacrity, for Lucifer had

become the most important thing on her horizon. He had a natural jump and he enjoyed it, and he gave Fiona a wonderful feeling of power and strength as he jumped. He learned quickly, and his fairly short stride enabled him to be clever and manoeuverable in his approaches.

"Blest if that isn't the most likely-looking show jumper I've seen for years," remarked the Colonel as he stood and watched the schooling session one afternoon. "I think we'll have him in the jumping field on the lunge to-morrow and see what he can do."

"If he really shows promise it would be worthwhile entering him in the novice classes at some of the local shows," suggested Gavin.

Fiona was thrilled to find that Lucifer came up to everybody's expectations.

"He loves it, too, which is more than half the battle," said the Colonel. "If he can clear five foot loose we can produce him as a show jumper. The only problem is—who's going to ride him? Fiona should, to be fair, but I'm not terribly keen to have two novices making their debut together. It's so easy to frighten a young horse—just get him tangled up in the furniture a few times and they start to stop."

"Give her a chance and see what she makes of it," Gavin suggested. "I really think he'll go better for her than he will for me, or anyone else for that matter. Besides, the fences are very low in the Foxhunter competitions. They are built for novice horses and novice riders, in order to encourage people to take their hunters into the ring. I've seen less experienced people than Fiona doing quite passably over those small courses."

"Well, we'll see how it goes. She and the horse understand one another, so it may not end in tears."

The Colonel was a firm believer in schooling horses thoroughly on the flat, to make them supple and obedient, before they were asked to leave the ground, so Fiona put in two hours a day in the school with Lucifer, under Mrs. Anstruther's eagle eye. The Colonel's wife took her dressage very seriously, and had taken numerous courses under a famous Continental instructor. Fiona was surprised how much she enjoyed her work, and she marvelled at the improvement which was wrought in the horse almost daily. Endless circling and changing rein, lengthening and shortening his stride and working on two tracks would not, a few weeks ago, have seemed particularly exciting. Now, however, that it was a means to an end, Fiona found it quite enthralling.

This was not merely dressage for its own sake, but dressage to train a horse to win jumping competitions. As she felt Lucifer becoming increasingly responsive, strong and fit beneath her it all seemed suddenly worthwhile. Temperamentally, too, he was a reformed character, and she no longer expected him to buck her into kingdom come whenever he twitched an ear.

By now he was jumping four foot with ease in the school, and he could stand well off both spread fences and uprights. Between the fences he was as handy as a polo pony, for he was naturally well-balanced, and he had learned how to deal with a simple double, whether the distance between its elements were long or short. When they tried him, with some trepidation, outside in the field, he went just as well as he had in the school.

"Half the professional riders in the country would bid me for him, if they saw him now!" laughed the Colonel delightedly one particularly successful afternoon. "Don't worry, though, Fiona! I wouldn't sell him now. I think we may well have an open jumper here, not just a promising novice. I wouldn't mind riding him myself."

"There's a small show over at South Leach early next month," said Mrs. Anstruther. "They sent me a schedule this morning. I'll put him in for the Foxhunter competition. Do you want any of the others to go?"

"There's really only Lindsay's horse with show jumping aspirations. She seems to be determined to jump him, though I think it's a waste of time and money. He'll never make a show jumper in a million years."

"She ought really to point-to-point him," said Gavin. "That would certainly be his *métier* if he were only a safer jumper. I looked up his record 'chasing the other day, though, and he fell more often than he finished."

Lindsay, however, seemed to have set her heart on turning Glenurquhart into a show jumper. She brought him in to join Lucifer's schooling sessions and was apparently quite undaunted by the fact that, though certainly bold enough, he did not seem to mind how much punishment he inflicted upon himself as he crashed through heavy poles with his knees and shins.

"He'll learn," she told Fiona confidently. "You'll see, he'll come all of a sudden. He's a very high-class horse, and high couraged. Of course, jumping fences flat, at speed, is a very different thing from jumping them slowly with an arched back. He can't be expected to change his style in five minutes. It's a pretty crummy sport anyway, compared to hunting or 'chasing. Still, I suppose it's something to do in the summer."

Fiona wondered secretly whether Lindsay's sudden and inordinate interest in this "crummy sport" was inspired by a grim determination to beat her and Lucifer, or whether it was simply a ruse to gain Gavin's attention. If it was the latter, she could not have been altogether satisfied with the results for Gavin's attention did not turn out to be very flattering. He was constantly holding forth on the utter futility of attempting to turn her horse into a show jumper, while Lucifer could do no wrong in his eyes. The rivalry between the two girls increased as the weeks went past.

"I wish I knew what this was all in aid of," remarked Elizabeth one day as she and Fiona bicycled side by side into the village to do some shopping. "I'm not altogether sure that I like it. I've a horrid feeling that she's got something rather unpleasant up her sleeve. I wish you were rooming with me instead—I can't imagine why Mrs. Anstruther put you with her."

"I don't think they know what she's really like. We'll ask to be together next term, though. In the meantime, I can stand another few weeks. Easter's early this year!"

The tension mounted during the last week before the South Leach Show. Fiona's sleep was disturbed every night by the oddest dreams, in all of which she was jumping an endless succession of incredibly high fences. Sometimes the dreams assumed the proportions of a nightmare as she knocked down every red and white pole, or fell off, or was responsible for Lucifer getting into serious trouble and injuring himself at a combination fence. They never had happy endings, and there was never a sign of a rosette, a prize card or a silver cup.

Lindsay, meanwhile, had taken herself and Glenurquhart away every evening on some mysterious expedition. Each one lasted for a couple of hours, and when they returned the horse looked excited and distressed. On the morning following one of these excursions he had a large lump on one knee.

"He hit it on a stone wall," Lindsay explained. "He's jumping much better, though. With any luck we may jump a clear round on Saturday."

On the morning of the show Fiona awoke before it was light and heard the stable clock striking four, five and six. Then she got up and pulled on the new breeches—which were sufficiently well-cut to be met with even Lindsay's approval—and a pair of woollen stockings. She knew, by now, that hunting boots are excruciatingly uncomfortable to walk around in for any length of time, and she intended to leave them off until she arrived at the show.

Lindsay slumbered on, and Fiona marvelled at her composure as she went downstairs and out into the stable yard. She was the first arrival, and a chorus of whinnies greeted her, shrill with delighted surprise. The hours were so regular at Wellesley Hall that each horse seemed to know to the minute when it was time for a feed.

Lucifer knuckered throatily at her as she entered his box. He, too, seemed perfectly calm and relaxed, and he attacked his first feed of the day with obvious enjoyment.

As she was mucking out the loosebox Gavin appeared.

"You're up bright and early!" he greeted her approvingly. "Couldn't you sleep?"

"Not very well," Fiona admitted. "I wish it were to-morrow morning—I've got terrible dentist's pains!"

"No need to have. Just forget about all the people and the fact that it's a competition and pretend you're jumping in the field here. And don't even think about winning. It'll be a miracle if you do, when it's the first time for either of you. There'll be plenty more shows during the summer."

Lindsay appeared soon afterwards, and then the three of them had an early breakfast and loaded the horses into the horse-box. The Colonel and his wife were to go later in the car.

"Give them plenty of work when you get there," the Colonel advised them. "They won't settle down if they're too fresh. The Foxhunter competition doesn't start until ten, so you've got plenty of time. Gavin, walk the course with them beforehand and let them know what they're in for. I don't imagine they'll find anything very startling. Roscoe Maxwell's building the course and he puts up very fair fences."

As they drove along in the cab of the horse-box with Gavin at the wheel, Fiona was feeling almost sick with excitement. It was a beautiful sunny morning in early spring, with still a slight nip in the air, and a gentle wind was blowing across the Cotswolds."

"You're lucky to-day," commented Gavin. "Last year it simply poured for the South Leach Show. The going was awful—they were up to their hocks in mud by the end of the day—and people were falling about like nine-pins. To-day the going should be very near perfect."

As they drew near to the field where the show was being held they got caught up in a convoy of horse-boxes and trailers. Some of them were towing caravans.

"It looks as though all the travelling circuses are on the move already," Gavin remarked. "They must be going on to another show afterwards. It's very early in the season, surely?"

"The professionals always get out on the road as early as they can," said Lindsay. "I shouldn't have thought they'd have bothered with a show of this size, though."

"There's a first prize of £25 in the open class. That's probably what's brought them here. They'll all have a novice or two as well—competition's going to be pretty hot to-day, girls, I'm afraid."

They drove through a rutted gateway, beyond which they could see the roped-off ring full of brightly painted fences. Then they trundled slowly up the field and parked at the end of a line of horse-boxes by the hedge. Already there were horses being ridden about the field and popped backwards and forwards over the practice jump at the side of the collecting ring.

Some of the riders, Fiona observed with a rapidly sinking heart, looked very professional indeed. They wore racing boots with their breeches and their horses were accoutred in all manner of unusual and—to Fiona—impressive devices, ranging from drop-nosebands and very tight standing martingales to various forms of running reins.

"Strapped up like so many suitcases," remarked Gavin derisively. "That's the sort of thing you have to do when you can't find the time or the energy to school a horse properly on the flat. It gets worse, of course, as time goes on, for when a horse builds up a defence against one set of artificial devices you have to set to to find a new lot—and so it continues until you have almost more leather than horse."

"But why do all these people do it?" asked Fiona.

"Because they are riding green horses which

they have bought during the winter, which they want to sell quickly for as large a profit as they can make. The horses, poor devils, never have a chance. They go from bad to worse and in a couple of years of being messed about they're almost useless."

"There's Ned Edwards," remarked Lindsay suddenly, indicating a lean, dark-featured man who was riding a bay gelding of the hunt-servant's type towards them.

"Now that's a real horseman," said Gavin, with a note of respect in his voicc. "No fancy bits and pieces for him, you notice—just a snaffle and a pair of hands. He has forgotten more about the art of jumping fences than most people ever knew."

Fiona was transfixed. She had seen Ned Edwards jumping at Wembley on her visits with with Miss Dodd, and she knew that he was the best professional in the country. Then she realised with a sudden rush of dismay that she would be competing against him in an hour or so, and her temerity appalled her.

The same thought had apparently occurred to Gavin. "Come on," he said. "Let's get the horses out and warm them up. Then I'll go down to the secretary's tent and get your numbers."

Both the horses had travelled quietly enough, but now Lindsay's 'chaser was peering around him with wildly rolling eyes and apparently imagining himself back at a race meeting. Gavin gave Lindsay a leg up and sent her away.

"That lunatic horse will only upset Lucifer if he hangs about here," he told Fiona. Lucifer was already looking about with considerable interest, that might well turn into excitement with the slightest encouragement. "Keep him away from the others as much as you can," he continued. "Try to keep him quiet and get him to settle, and I'll be back soon."

Lucifer remained outwardly sensible, although he was very much on his toes, and Fiona was relieved to find that he responded to her readily enough. She rode him about for half an hour or so until Gavin beckoned her down to the collecting ring.

"We'll give him a pop, just to remind him what he's here for, and then you'd better prepare for action! You're drawn to jump second."

Fiona grimaced. "Oh well, I suppose it's better to get it over with than just to keep hanging about."

Gavin nodded. "Far less nerve-racking. Now, take him over that post and rails and then keep him on the move in the collecting ring. When the first rider goes, start cantering. If you let a horse go into the ring half-asleep, you ask for all you get."

Lucifer cantered down to the practice fence with his usual measured stride, took off boldly and jumped it cleanly and well with his back arched like a bow. Fiona felt a rush of cautious confidence as she patted his shoulder.

"That'll do us," grinned Gavin. "If he jumps all the other fences as well as that it'll be a good beginning."

First in the order of jumping was Ned Edwards. Fiona was too busy keeping Lucifer cantering, according to instructions, to watch his round, but she heard the announcer say: "last rider—clear round!" and she knew that she had a high standard to follow.

Once in the ring she was surprised how easy it was to forget the occasion and the spectators. The only important things were Lucifer and the fences that she saw between his ears. For the rest, she might indeed have been schooling in the field at home.

The first fence was a low brush with an ox-rail superimposed. Lucifer put it flippantly behind him and Fiona steadied him as he cantered on to the next fence without altering his stride. When that was safely behind them she began to enjoy herself, and one by one they made their way triumphantly round the course. There was an anxious moment at the double when Lucifer stood off too far and landed short, but he was clever enough to keep out of trouble and Fiona was wise enough to give him the chance. He put in an extra stride and twisted like a cat over the last element.

Fiona was almost bursting with pride when she left the ring with "clear round" echoing in her ears.

"Well done you!" exclaimed a beaming Gavin, patting Lucifer ecstatically. "Do you want to have a crack at the jump-off? I'm not sure that you two haven't done enough for one day on your first outing."

"Oh, please!"

"All right, then. Where on earth d'you suppose Lindsay's got to? I've hardly seen her since we arrived. She's not due to jump for some time yet, but she ought to be down here ready."

Fiona had a shrewd suspicion that Lindsay might be with the hunting farmer whose box she had recognised at the top of the field, but she said nothing. Then a voice behind her said: "Your horse jumped a nice round, miss. He was lucky at the double, but too big a stand-off's a good fault."

Looking around, she saw Ned Edwards smiling at her, and her cup was full. She was later to discover that it was his habit to watch every single horse jumping every single fence in order that he might know which were worth buying and which were not, but now she was sure that he had noticed Lucifer particularly because he was so outstanding.

It was an easy course, specially built to get the horses going well and give them confidence at the beginning of the season, and the clear rounds began to accumulate until they became the rule rather than the exception. Not that this detracted from Fiona's happiness in the slightest. She rode over to where Gavin was standing, looking slightly worried and annoyed at Lindsay's continuing absence.

"He is super, isn't he?" she said again.

"Quite brilliant!" laughed the Colonel, strolling up behind them. "No, all joking apart, he went very well indeed for the first time. Now, where's our other representative?"

"Blessed if I know. Vanished off the face of the earth, by the look of it." Just then a harrassed-looking official hurried over to them.

"Colonel Anstruther," he began, considerably embarrassed, "May I please have a word with you in private? Something rather distressing has happened, I'm afraid."

The Colonel, looking perplexed, withdrew a few paces. The steward spoke in low tones, but Fiona could see his listener's face getting more and more serious. "Thank you," he said finally. "I'll deal with this situation. I am very sorry indeed that it has occurred."

"What's up, Father?" asked Gavin.

"Someone's reported Lindsay to the stewards," said Colonel Anstruther grimly. "Apparently she's up there in the horse lines with some farmer feller, and they've been chucking everything but the kitchen stove at that wretched horse of hers. I wondered about that knee the other day. She must have been rapping him for weeks, poor devil. This is a very serious matter. Then he started refusing and they really set about him. I shouldn't be surprised if the R.S.P.C.A. doesn't take a hand in this."

Fiona listened, horrified, while the story was unfolded. She had heard, vaguely, about people doing cruel things to horses' legs in order to make them pick them up higher when they were jumping.

"What were they using?" asked Gavin, quietly furious.

"A chain and an iron bar, I gather. And the horse has weals on him where they knocked him about when he refused. I'm afraid she'll have to go. I'll telephone her father to-night. Darling," he added, turning to his wife, "go and find her and take her back in the car, will you? It's too bad to spoil Fiona's day too. She can ride in the jump-off and then I'll come home in the box. Gavin, you'd better go and see to that poor devil of a horse. Load him up so that as few people as possible can see him. People who don't know us may get the impression that that's the way we school our horses."

Fiona was too upset to achieve another clear round in the jump-off, though Lucifer only trailed one hind toe over the brick wall and they did not disgrace themselves with four faults.

"Never mind," said the Colonel consolingly as they returned to the collecting ring. "There's bound to be another jump-off, and against the clock, too. Lucifer's really done enough for to-day, and I don't approve of chasing inexperienced horses around before they know what they're doing at their own speed. There's always another day, you know, my dear."

A remarkably subdued Lindsay was packing her things when Fiona, having attended to Lucifer's comfort, returned to her room.

"I'll be glad to get out of this place," she said sullenly. "My father's coming to take me home to-morrow."

"What about Glenurquhart?" asked Fiona. She had helped Gavin to unload him and put him in his box, and been sickened by the marks on his side and the horse's nervous condition.

"Useless brute—I daresay we'll sell him," said Lindsay coldly. "He's got the wrong temperament for a show jumper. If you set about him he packs up."

"I don't blame him," declared Fiona indignantly. "I don't know how you could allow a horse to be treated like that."

She got into bed and thought of Lucifer and how well he had gone that day. All the weeks of patient schooling had paid high dividends, and she was sure that this was only the beginning. That night she dreamt of red rosettes and silver cups and of honour and glory for the former problem horse that she had fallen in love with when first she saw him with the other colts in the field.

CHAPTER VII

A Red Rosette

THE SUMMER passed like wildfire. Fiona was so busy that she hardly had time to think. In addition to all her ordinary work, she was preparing for the British Horse Society's instructor's examination, which would enable her to get a good teaching job when she left Wellesley Hall at the end of the summer. She was also continuing with Lucifer's schooling, and almost every Saturday she and Gavin took him off to compete at some show in the neighbourhood.

The young horse was gaining in experience and ability with each outing, and he had already created quite an impression among the knowledgable-looking men who gathered in the collecting ring at every show. Several of them had asked the Colonel what he would take for him.

"Sorry!" the latter replied, "but he's not for sale. We have high hopes of him, and he may be worth a lot of money one day."

Lucifer had already won several rosettes in Foxhunter competitions, and on one exciting day he finished second to a very well-known lady rider on a German-bred horse which was reputed to have won competitions on the Continent already, though no one was able to prove it.

"He shouldn't be classified as a novice at all," said Gavin. "Funny the lengths some people will go to, just to win a few easy pounds. Never mind, Lucifer, old boy. Your day will come, you'll see."

It came the very next week—and at the big show at Meltonham where they had not expected to do especially well. Fiona had never ridden at such a big show before, and she knew that the competition would be very stiff. Nor was she wrong. Two international riders had brought novices with them to jump in the Foxhunter competition, and there were several well-known national riders whose horses could be depended upon to put up a good show.

"The course won't be as easy to-day as those we've met before," Gavin announced as he came back from declaring his entry at the secretary's tent. "Michael Davenport's designed it, and he delights in building rather tricky fences to reduce the number of clear rounds and speed up the programme."

Fiona, however, was gaining confidence by this time, both in herself and in the bay horse. As she walked the course with Gavin she felt that, provided both she and Lucifer kept their heads, they could easily manage to jump it clear. There were several twists and turns, and a horse would have to be moderately manoeuvrable, but all Lucifer's basic training would now stand him in good stead.

It was a glorious June day, so warm that people were riding around in their shirtsleeves and only donning their coats in time to enter the ring. Everything was pervaded by the sharp, fresh smell of grass, bruised by iron-shod feet. The bright green of the turf, the snowy white of the tents and marquees, and the bay, grey, brown and chestnut of the gleaming-coated horses under the bright blue sky made of the scene a Munnings picture. Its beauty nearly took Fiona's breath away, and Lucifer, too, was drinking in every detail as he gazed around him. Suddenly he knuckered delightedly, and following his eyes, Fiona saw a mare with a very small foal at foot being led past. Lucifer, suddenly excited, did his best to follow them.

"Silly fellow!" smiled Fiona, patting him. "That's not yours! Its mother would probably send you flying if you went anywhere near."

"Odd how geldings seem to love foals," Gavin remarked. "We once had one who was a regular menace—kept jumping into the field with the brood mares. Why, there's a horse I recognise. Where have I seen it before?"

Fiona looked around and gasped. "Why, it's Glenurquhart!" she gasped. "Lindsay must have sold him—she said she was going to. Who's that riding him?"

"That's Syd Jenkins—the farmer who was knocking him about that day. He always has a few jumpers in the summer and he's a fair horseman, but he isn't exactly noted for his humanity. Wonder what he's done to that poor old horse? It'll be interesting to see how he goes."

They did not have long to speculate, for Glenurquhart was early in the jumping order. He was leaner and harder than he had been in the Spring, but he looked well, and apart from a tight standing martingale he wore no odd contrivances. As he cantered into the ring with a burly-looking rider on board and jumped the first fence, Fiona marvelled at the difference in his style.

"Why, he's got him to bend his back!" she exclaimed. "He doesn't flatten any more, does he?"

"No," admitted Gavin, "But he's terribly careful now. Remember how bold he was? Now he's barely cantering into his fences, and he'd turn himself inside out to avoid hitting one. I hate to see a horse jumping like that. Looks as though he's half-frightened at what's going to happen to him if he touches a pole."

Glenurquhart jumped rather a sticky clear round and left the ring. "What do you think will become of him?" asked Fiona.

"Oh, he'll win a few competitions this summer and then get sold before he is upgraded. Some girl will buy him, probably—he's a nice-looking horse—and he'll never be heard of again. He's never an open jumper—if he goes on jumping he'll still be a novice five years from now."

The next in the ring was a young man who had shot into the limelight the previous season with a big grey horse and jumped for Britain at two international shows. His novice was also a grey, big and rather lumbering, a reasonably useful Irishman with a fair amount of draught horse in his veins.

"I wouldn't give much for my chances of survival if that one fell on me out hunting!" laughed Gavin. "He jumps, though, by golly. Here's another clear round coming up."

After this there was quite a lot of crashing timber before the second international rider, a grim-looking young woman with a face that reminded Fiona of Punch. She was riding a little chestnut Anglo-Arab mare with a white face like a Hereford cow and a wildly rolling eye. They jumped a fast and fluent clear round and left the ring to a round of applause. Then there was a rush of children, swarming around the little mare for her rider's autograph.

"Three clear rounds," said Gavin, "and only about five more to jump. I told you they'd be sorted out to-day, Fiona. Mind you're not among the victims!"

One more horse went, and then it was Fiona's

turn. Lucifer knew by now what was expected of him, and he cantered into the ring with his ears cocked, prepared for battle. He jumped the course smoothly and steadily and his rider had never an anxious moment from start to finish. She left the ring flushed with triumph. Lucifer had never gone better, and he felt so powerful beneath her that she almost believed he would jump a house if she asked him.

"Well done," said Gavin quietly. "We've come through the first round unscathed. Three inches more shouldn't make much difference to him now."

Fiona glanced over at Glenurquhart as the stewards put the fences up. The horse was sweating and glancing anxiously around him. She hoped for his sake that he, too, would jump another clear round, but he was eliminated at the wall.

The young man on the big grey went clear again, and so did the young woman on the chestnut mare. Then it was Fiona's turn, and once again Lucifer turned up trumps. He gave her an anxious moment when he came too close to one fence, putting in an extra stride and taking off almost underneath it, but he corkscrewed in mid-air and somehow got himself out of trouble.

"That was a close shave!" she admitted to Gavin, who was talking to the Anglo-Arab's rider.

"Now, don't forget that the next round is on

time, over the same course. Don't gallop flat out and unbalance him, but go the shortest way. It's between the fences that you win this sort of finish, not over them!"

The grey horse jumped a third clear round, but his time of 44 seconds was not particularly fast. The chestnut mare went like the wind, but flicked a pole off the very last fence when she seemed certain to win.

"Now, the luck of the draw favours you," Gavin told Fiona. "You saw how slowly the grey horse went. Don't take any chances, but go a little faster. Good luck to you."

Lucifer seemed to know exactly what was required of him, and he turned on the tap of his own accord, and Fiona found the shortest distance from A to B with almost geometrical precision. Their clear round, which was never in doubt, was achieved in 37⅕ seconds, making them easy winners. Fiona felt dazed as she returned to the collecting ring.

"You've done it, by Jove! Jolly good show!" Gavin greeted her, and people she barely knew by sight came up to congratulate her. As she stood in the centre of the ring a moment later while the local M.P.'s wife fumblingly attached a red rosette to Lucifer's bridle, her joy was complete. Lucifer was going to be an international horse some day, of that there could be no doubt!

On the way home she leaned dreamily back in

the uncomfortable front seat of the horse-box and re-lived each moment again. Gavin cast a tolerant grin in her direction.

"What are you thinking of—the Queen Elizabeth Cup? You know, don't you, that now you've qualified Lucifer for the regional final of the Foxhunter competition? He only has to win that—or get in the first three—and you can ride him at the Horse of the Year show at Wembley. How does that appeal?"

Fiona looked ecstatic, and then suddenly she said: "When is the regional final?"

"I don't know—sometime in September, I think. Why, what's the matter?"

Fiona groaned. "But I shan't be here then. My course finishes this term, you know. By September, provided I've got my diploma, of course, I hope to be in a job."

"That's dreadful—we'll have to see that you fail your exam! Would that do any good?"

"I'm afraid not. It'd probably mean my being whisked off to some place or other. I don't think my parents would let me stay here for another year—they don't really approve of horses, you know."

"Some people don't," agreed Gavin, still bantering. "So you've got to pass that exam and get a job quickly if you're to remain in touch?"

"That's about it. But who will ride Lucifer when I go?"

"I might have a shot at it myself. I must admit I've been longing to for quite a long time."

If only, Fiona thought, she had enough money to buy Lucifer. She made up her mind to save every penny she could, though she knew in her heart that if he was half as good as she imagined him to be he would be so expensive that even a whisker would be beyond her reach.

By now, she and Elizabeth had achieved their ambition of sharing a room. From the work point of view it was a mixed blessing, for Elizabeth took nothing seriously and insisted on talking whenever Fiona was trying to study; but from every other aspect if was eminently satisfactory to both of them.

"I wonder what's happened to Lindsay?" remarked Fiona idly as they chatted together that evening. "We saw that poor horse of hers to-day. He's been bought by that farmer friend of Lindsay's."

"Oh, I expect her father's packed her off somewhere else by now. They didn't get on at all, you know. Maybe that's why Lindsay's so hard. She has a loathsome stepmother, too, who can't be bothered with her. I expect she'll soon marry someone perfectly ghastly just to get away from home."

"She needn't," said Fiona. "She's very good-looking. I should think she'll marry someone quite presentable."

"Yes, but—didn't you notice?—she always seemed to prefer rather tough sort of men? And yet in many ways she was a tremendous snob. Funny girl—I never understood her."

As July examination time drew near the pace began to quicken, and there was very little time for shows. More as a matter of form than anything else the girls also had to be examined on their prowess with a rolling pin and a needle and their ability to speak and write reasonable French. Not caring in the slightest how she fared in any of these tests, Fiona was startled to find herself emerging with flying colours. She interpreted her success as an extremely bad omen that was bound to result in a dismal failure in the one thing that mattered to her, the British Horse Society's exam.

On the first of the fateful three days two benign old cavalry officers of uncertain vintage arrived on the evening train. They were the cynosure of all eyes as they dined that night at the Anstruthers' table.

"Why two?" queried Fiona.

"One for the actual practical work, one for theory, perhaps," suggested Elizabeth. "I don't know. Eat up your nice institution food or you'll be too weak to give the right answers to-morrow!"

Fiona grimaced and attacked her processed ham and potato salad. "I hope they're enjoying the salmon mousse I made this afternoon."

That night she made Elizabeth ask her all sorts

of obscure questions gleaned from an old veterinary manual—an impressive tome which weighed a ton and had educated previous generations of Army cadets.

"It's ghastly how many different things horses can suffer from," she sighed. "I can't even pronounce most of them, let alone treat them."

"Well, you aren't supposed to be depriving the vets of their means of livelihood," replied Elizabeth consolingly. "We're only supposed to concern ourselves with minor ailments. Anything more complicated calls for professional attention. When in doubt, call the vet."

"How I shall remember anything at all tomorrow I really don't know," said Fiona dismally. "I wish it were all over—I'm a nervous wreck already. If they give me that excruciatingly uncomfortable Mistinguett to ride I shall collapse on the spot."

"You'll probably get Lucifer, so don't worry," Elizabeth reassured her. "The Anstruthers are as anxious for you to get your certificate as you are, you know—especially as it's now or never, and your parents won't send you back for another year whatever happens. The more pupils who turn out successfully, the better it is for the school's reputation."

The two old men looked slightly less benevolent the following morning, but Fiona's confidence returned in some measure when she found that, true to her friend's prediction, she had been put down to ride Lucifer in the practical test. She rode in the school to the commands issued from the gallery by the judges, and she could not help but know that she put up a good show. The Colonel, who was sitting behind the examiners, smiled at her approvingly as she finished.

"Right, Fiona. Send in the next one, and report to the stables after lunch for the stable management exam."

"I made an awful hash of my practical," groaned Elizabeth at lunch. "You know how hopeless Nimrod is at a turn on the haunches? His hind legs shot out in every direction, and then he insisted on a counter-lead right round the school. As far as I can see, I'm here for the duration."

"Duration of what?" smiled Fiona.

"My life, I expect! My family are quite happy in the knowledge that I am leading a nice, healthy, wholesome life."

"Well, we're none of us likely to be made wards of court in these surroundings!" remarked another girl with a laugh.

"Can anyone tell me what lymphangitis is?" asked Fiona in a sudden panic. "My mind's a complete blank."

"It's something you'll never be in danger of contracting here," answered Elizabeth drily. "Filled legs, overheated blood and sometimes temporary paralysis, caused by eating too much highly-concentrated food accompanied by lack of work!"

The questions, however, turned out to be comparatively easy, and the diagnosis of lymphangitis was not among them. Fiona did not feel that she had emerged from the exam too badly, though wild horses would not have dragged from her a confession of optimism as to the outcome.

When the results came through, however, she found that she had done even better than she had hoped.

"You've passed, with flying colours, my dear," the Colonel told her after breakfast one morning. "In fact, you're our star pupil. Considering how little you knew when you came here you have done us great credit, and we're very proud of your progress."

"What are your plans, when you leave here?" asked Mrs. Anstruther.

"I shall have a holiday with my family first, and then I'm going to advertise for a job," replied Fiona.

"Well, we shall miss you. Perhaps you'll come back and see us sometimes—and Lucifer."

Fiona was not looking forward to leaving Wellesley Hall, where she had been so happy, but still less did she relish the prospect of losing Lucifer. Gavin promised to send her a telegram if the horse managed to qualify for the finals of the Foxhunter competition at Wembley, but the thought of anyone else riding him, even Gavin, saddened her. However unreasonably, she had come to regard him as her own property.

Her family was going to Scotland for the summer, and before she left with them Fiona put an advertisement in "Horse and Hound". The number of replies she got astounded her.

"Whatever accomplishments did you list?" demanded Miles incredulously. "There must be a tremendous shortage of girl grooms, or whatever you call yourself."

The replies came from as far afield as Ireland, and Fiona was sorely tempted to go and work for a husband and wife who had just taken on the Mastership of a pack of hounds in Co. Cork. From some friends in the same county, however, the indefatigable Aunt Helen had elicted the information that the new Master and his wife drank too much, fought like cat and dog and owed money to most of the horse dealers in the South of Ireland, so the job was firmly vetoed. Fiona had to admit to herself that, although she would be certain to get as much exciting hunting as she wanted, she would be able to do no instructing at all in such a job. Indeed, apart from making young horses and probably taking some crucifying falls while they learned to jump enormous banks, she would not be able to use many of her hard-won qualifications.

She refused her services to a peculiar-sounding riding school on the outskirts of Birmingham, who advertised "late evening classes for office workers" upon their prospectus; and, more reluctantly, to a dealer in Leicestershire who required her to accompany him on horse-coping trips to various sales up and down the country. It sounded rather fun, but her father condemned it out of hand as most unsuitable. "I will not have you associating with thieves and rogues at horse fairs while I still have breath in my body. And nor will I have you traipsing around the countryside with one of them."

"Jed Marsh has got a good reputation as a dealer," protested Fiona mildly.

"So has the man I buy my cars from, but I wouldn't trust him with my only daughter," replied her father firmly.

There were numerous letters from harrassed mothers, offering her the dubious privilege of "living as a family."

"That means," Aunt Helen said darkly, "that you will be nanny, part-time cook, chauffeur and groom to your employers—you may even have to do a bit of gardening and milk the house cow as well. If I were you I'd find a nice riding school in an attractive part of the world—as much like Wellesley Hall as you can find. You'll have a far nicer time and make many more friends than you would in any of these other jobs."

The opportunity seemed to present itself in the letter from the Moorview Riding School and Stud Farm on the edge of Dartmoor. Its proprietor, a Mrs. Prendergast, required a qualified instructress to prepare resident pupils for the British Horse Society's certificate. Fiona learned that she would be able to hunt on Dartmoor, to ride young horses, broken at the establishment, in local shows, and to help with the supervision of the brood mares that were sent each Spring to the stud's two thoroughbred and one pony stallions. It sounded ideal, and even Fiona's conscientious relations could find no fault with the situation.

Thus it was that, early in September, Fiona found herself catching an Exeter-bound train at Paddington, full of excitement at the prospect of her first job. She had been appointed an assistant instructress at a salary of three pounds a week, plus commission and keep.

"Whatever is that supposed to mean?" Miles demanded.

"Perhaps it's a commission on selling horses," replied Fiona hopefully. But she was later to discover that it was a very rare occurrence indeed for Mrs. Prendergast to succeed in selling any of her horses—certainly no one who lived in the vicinity ever wanted to buy them—and the exact nature of the commission was destined to remain a mystery as long as Fiona remained in Devonshire.

Mrs. Prendergast was not at the station to meet

her. Instead, a rickety old van was awaiting her, driven by a long-haired youth whose mental capacity seemed to be very limited. Fiona was somewhat perplexed by the information that he "tended the bar", and she wondered what kind of establishment she was entering. She was very soon to find out.

CHAPTER VIII

Devonshire

The Moorview Riding School and its proprietress were something of a joke throughout South Devon. Mrs. Prendergast was, it was generally admitted, utterly devoted to horses and exemplary in her care of them, but she always had far too many of them and was invariably short of money. In order to buy corn and hay she took in working pupils whom she consistently overworked, she kept horses at livery, and she had turned the downstairs part of her large, rambling, ramshackle old house into licensed premises.

Thus, when Fiona arrived in the front seat of the old grey van, jolting along the rutted lane with its high bank on either side, she was quite unprepared for the sight which met her eyes. It could not have provided more of a contrast with Wellesley Hall.

An inn sign, painted by a very amateurish hand and depicting a most improbable horse jumping an astronomical stone wall, hung above the oak-studded front door of a long, low house of pink-washed cob. Sitting outside at an old-fashioned wooden table, with large glass tankards in their hands, was a collection of gaitered old men, their voices raised in song. To remain in character they should have been singing "Widecombe Fair" or some equally bucolic ditty, but Fiona was dismayed to recognise the strains of a modern Country and Western ballad, singularly out of keeping both with the singers and their surroundings.

Adjoining the house was a line of loose-boxes, each with its occupant's head gazing indifferently out at the revellers. They seemed to consist of cobs, for the most part, with here and there a pony and the odd character which defied categorical description. Dogs lay about all over the placc—at a rough guess Fiona estimated that there must be five or six—and a collection of hybrid chickens scratched their way about the yard. Lying near the table where the men were slaking their thirst was the largest, most indecent-looking pinkish-white pig that she had ever seen.

Her driver stopped the van with a flourish that made the dust fly and nearly catapulted his passenger through the windscreen. At that moment a wiry, bird-like, ageless little woman came through the front door carrying a steaming pail of mash. She was wearing an antiquated pair of whitish corduroy trousers with enormously baggy legs, and a faded blue aertex shirt with a stringy tie. Her face was deeply lined and burned walnut-coloured by the sun, and her greying hair was scraped back and pushed into a net. She had the brightest, most piercing, blue eyes that it was possible to imagine.

"You must be Fiona," she said as she advanced, holding out a gnarled and bony hand. "My husband will show you your room, and then you can come and see the horses. Cyril! Come and take the new girl to her room."

A colourless little man, as wizened as his wife, appeared from within the house and nodded absently at Fiona. She was later to discover that he was a kindly person, completely devoid of either character or accomplishments and absolutely dominated by his wife. Oddly enough, they got on very well together. She regarded him with tolerant affection, while he both doted and depended upon her utterly.

She followed him into the low-ceilinged farmhouse hall, whose walls were covered with faded photographs of horses, and up the narrow stairs, while the boy came behind with her suitcases. The upstairs landing was bumpy and uneven and the floorboards creaked with age. The walls were whitewashed and the bedroom doors were finished in a nondescript brown stain. Mr. Prendergast led the way to a room at the far end of a long corridor.

"I do hope you'll be comfortable," he said kindly, opening the door on a tiny cupboard of a room containing the bare essentials—a lumpy-looking bed, a disreputable chest of drawers surmounted by a mirror and a straight-backed cane chair. Inadequate, faded gingham curtains framed the little window, and a length of the same material was suspended from one corner of the room to do duty as a makeshift wardrobe. As it was cheerless even in late summer, Fiona shivered at the vision it would present on a cold winter night—especially as there was no obvious form of heating—but it was her first job, she was young and enthusiastic so she simply replied:

"Thank you very much. I'm sure I shall. Do you change for dinner?"

"Bless you, no, we don't stand on ceremony here! Just get into jodhpurs or slacks, as you please. I'll leave you to unpack your things, and then my wife will be waiting for you out in the stables."

When he had gone Fiona sallied forth to find the bathroom. After she had opened three wrong doors she came across it, right at the top of the stairs. The bath was ringed with a series of tide-marks left by previous bathers, and a dingy-looking, torn bath-mat hung over its edge. The washbasin was small and cracked and surrounded by half-finished pieces of soap. The wooden lavatory seat was so scratched as to be virtually devoid of varnish, and the checkered linoleum was worn into holes. Fiona, who had a penchant for glamorous bathrooms with shining tiles and all-over carpeting, found this one too comfortless and depressing for words.

Later she put on a shirt and a pair of twill trousers and went down to the stable. The house appeared to be deserted, though through a half-open door in the hall downstairs she could see the bar, behind which stood her employer, reading a paper. Outside in the yard the old men, no longer singing, stared at her curiously.

"Good evening," she volunteered.

" 'Evening, miss," they replied in chorus.

The stable was a hive of activity with clanking buckets and bustling figures emerging from every box. The building was old-fashioned, but Mrs. Prendergast was clearly far more particular in her stable management than she seemed to be in the running of her house. The horses were blooming with health, and up to their hocks in clean wheat straw.

She was on her knees beside a common-looking brown mare with its off-fore in a steaming bucket.

"This lady has given herself a leg," she explained. A knot of small girls who were gathered around the door of the box made way for Fiona. "This is Fiona, girls, my new assistant instructress. These, Fiona, are my working pupils —Angela, Jennifer, Marian, Jane and Christine. You'll discover for yourself which is which, by and by."

The working pupils were all younger than

Fiona and she did not expect to find them very companionable. She was relieved, however, that they seemed to be quite easy material for her to work on for the first time in her new capacity of instructress. They were gazing at her in considerable awe, and looked as though they would accept as gospel anything that she cared to tell them. She discovered later that they were dedicated beings, and they reminded her a little of herself before Wellesley Hall had widened her horizon. They worked extremely hard for their keep, plus a little pocket money each week. It was a beneficial arrangment on both sides, for they got a very thorough grounding in matters pertaining to the horse and Mrs. Prendergast got cheap and willing labour.

Soon the little band of helpers was gathered admiringly around Fiona while she showed them how to put on a poultice. By the time they had made everything shipshape—and Mrs. Prendergast kept them at it until there was not a straw out of place—dusk was falling. The little party in the yard had adjourned to the bar inside the house, and their employer marched her pupils into the kitchen.

One of the girls laid the long refectory table with a dingy piece of oilcloth, while another cooked bacon and eggs on the old-fashioned range. Yet another made an enormous pot of tea, and after they were joined by Mr. Prendergast, they all sat down to their evening meal. No one discussed anything but horses—and then only the horses belonging to the Moorview Stables—and nobody seemed to want to.

When the master of the house had finished his last slice of bread and jam he went off to the bar, and his place was taken by the bartender, whose name was apparently Jim. He ate voraciously, in complete silence, which Fiona found a little disconcerting until she realised that, as Jim was not a horseman, there was absolutely nothing that he could discuss in this horse-crazy household.

Fiona was not allowed to help with the washing-up, which did not unduly distress her, and as there seemed to be nothing else to do, and no place to sit except the kitchen or the bar, she went early to bed. Resolving to buy something with which to clean the bath the following day, she contented herself with a wash and retired to her room. But not to sleep. Her wakefulness was due in part to the amount of tea she had drunk, and in part to the fact that her bedroom seemed to be directly over the bar. The old walls and floors were thick, but she could still hear a constant buzz of conversation, while snatches of song floated in at the open window. Later, when the revellers had gone home, she was kept awake by shrill little shrieks and heavy scratching sounds which sounded ominously like rats. The next day she discovered that her room was right next door to the hay loft, and thereafter she lived in constant dread that a rat would find its way through the wall and pay her a visit.

She eventually fell asleep wondering why on earth she had come here, and how long she could stand it. She decided to give it a trial for a week, however, for she was unwilling to admit defeat so easily.

The household was astir at the crack of dawn, and one of the pupils brought her an unexpected and incredibly strong cup of tea shortly after six in the morning. Fiona emptied it surreptitiously down the wash-basin and went downstairs to find the kitchen deserted. The all-pervading smell of stale beer and smoke, which seeped out from the bar to permeate the entire downstairs premises, made her feel slightly nauseated, and she hurried out to the stables, where work had already begun.

And extremely hard work it was. By evening, she was exhausted by the combination of her labours and the soft, relaxing Devonshire air. She had ridden six young horses who were to be introduced to hounds the following morning, she had supervised spring-cleaning operations in a crowded, inadequate tack room and taken an inventory of its contents, and she had walked miles home with one of the stallions after an irate neighbouring farmer had telephoned to say that the horse had broken into his ten-acre field and was worrying his cart mares.

"These stallions of Mrs. Prendergast's are a proper nuisance, that they be," complained the farmer when Fiona arrived in the van, driven once again by the silent bartender, Jim. "Forever breaking out of their fields and wandering all over the countryside, once their mares have gone away at the end of the summer. Why don't she keep them in boxes as other folk do? Now, mind how you go with him, Miss. Proper brewed up, he be."

Apart from shying at his own reflection in the village shop window, however, and doing what felt like irreparable damage to her foot when he jumped on it, the old thoroughbred horse with his beautifully crested, powerful neck was amenable enough, and Fiona did not use the short stick that Mrs. Prendergast had thrust into her hand as she departed. He jogged along, playing with his bit and making occasional darts in her direction with his teeth bared alarmingly, but she soon discovered that there was no harm in him and that this was merely his way of enlivening the journey. He was a grand-looking horse, even now, when old age and a hard racing career had broken him down and thickened one tendon till his near-fore looked like a bolster. In his youth he must have been a picture.

"Thank goodness Androcles is all right," her employer greeted her as she arrived back in the yard, footsore and weary. "We have had him for ten years and he's had some wonderful foals—the old villain, breaking out again! Was Mr. Yeo very annoyed?"

"He was, rather. He said that other people keep their stallions in boxes."

"So they do, most of them. But we always let ours run out, and put the mares in with them when they arrive. We get over 77 per cent. of them in foal that way, and it saves us endless time and trouble. Also our stallions are never vicious or bad-tempered—why, any of my girls can handle them. Some people's stallions are positive man-eaters, and who can blame them, cooped up by themselves all the time and treated as dangerous animals. I wouldn't condemn any horse of mine to a life like that."

"Do you keep each stallion in a different field?" inquired Fiona, who found her employer unorthodox but interesting, and definitely knowledgeable.

"Of course, otherwise we'd have terrible fights." Mrs. Prendergast did not add that her fences were so bad that the horses often got inextricably mixed up during the night, and that a valuable point-to-point mare had once been sent to Androcles but had actually produced a pint-sized foal to the cream-coloured Welsh pony stallion.

The following morning everyone arose even earlier than they had the previous day, and it was still dark when Fiona made her way out to the stables to go cub-hunting. A sea-mist hovered breast-high over the valley, and the stars flickered still in the dawn-streaked sky. Once the effort of getting out of bed had been achieved it was a beautiful time of day.

An hour or so later, when the sun was just emerging over the hill-top behind the house, a little cavalcade set off to go cub-hunting. Each of the pupils was mounted on one of the young horses, who were all of the same stamp—short-legged, deep-bodied and plain, but workmanlike: typical West Country hunters in the making. Fiona had been put on a young blood horse for which his owner had point-to-pointing aspirations—a long-backed, mealy-brown animal with an apparently wooden neck and a mouth like iron, who rejoiced, paradoxically, in the name of The Saint. Mrs. Prendergast was riding a little blood weed of a chestnut mare, fussy and fidgety, which, she told Fiona, she was going to show as a hack the following summer.

The meet was on a village green some four miles distant, and Fiona noticed at once that, even taking into consideration the fact that this was only cub-hunting and that the season proper had not yet started, hunting in Devonshire was very different from its counterpart in the fashionable Cotswolds. The Master, a young man recently retired from the Army to agriculture, had taken over the pack from his father and hunted hounds himself. His whipper-in and kennel-huntsman was a hoary old ruffian called Tom Firkin who looked like Leech's conception of John Jorrocks and sat on his half-bred, fiddle-headed, hairy-heeled horse like a species of limpet attired in baggy fawn breeches, equally ill-fitting boots and a red coat that had faded to a dusty pink.

The field consisted for the most part of jovial-looking farmers in cloth caps and gum-boots, riding rough-looking horses which had been snatched in from their fields and pressed into service with the most cursory attention to their appearance. They were, nevertheless, as Fiona was to discover, a very sporting community who enjoyed their hunting every bit as much as those who were better mounted and more traditionally clad.

The hounds were a beautifully level lot, mostly lemon-pied, and Mrs. Prendergast told her that they had been in the Montague family for more than a hundred years and had been bred up from the old-fashioned West Country harriers.

"They hunt with a wonderful cry, and it takes a good horse to live with them on the moor. This morning, of course, you won't see them doing much but bustling the cubs around in covert, but we have a lot of fun once the season starts."

The young horses were staring at the pack with popping eyes, and the contingent from the Moorview Stables presented a somewhat unruly spectacle when the Master decided to move off and draw the covert they had passed as they rode into the village. It was a larch plantation, situated at the side of a very steep field, and the riders on their puffing, unfit horses made their way up to the very top, whence they could look down through the trees and see most of what was going on.

"There be three or four litters of cubs in this covert," one apple-cheeked farmer vouchsafed to another. "I see'd three on 'em only last week from the bedroom window. Young Captain Montague'll need to chop as many as he can this morning if we're to have any decent hunts from here this season."

"The young captain's like every other young man—wants to gallop and jump and show what he's made of," remarked the other. "No one'll be better pleased than he if a fox gets away to-day and gives us a run. Can't really say I'll be sorry myself, and I daresay old Bess'd like to stretch her legs," and he patted the carty black cob he was riding.

"You'd be sorry enough if your ewes were lambing in this field," retorted the other. "A hunt's supposed to kill foxes, not just go out to enjoy itself."

"No harm as I can see in doing both. Listen, will you, to that hound speaking! They'll be driving one out this end, surely to goodness."

Fiona, trying in vain to make her horse stand

still, craned her neck and peered into the larches. Suddenly she saw a slim red form making its way towards her. One of the farmers saw it too, almost simultaneously, and let out an ear-splitting holler, at the same time banging his saddle flap with the stock of his whip. Instantly the others started banging their saddles to get the fox to turn back, and all the young horses pretended to jump out of their skins with terror.

In the confusion that followed, another fox slipped away and broke covert on the far side. The pack divided in two, with the Master following the hounds which had elected to pursue the vagrant, while Tom Firkin remained behind to harry the first cub. The field, to a man, galloped off after their huntsman.

Fiona got away to a good start, but then she remembered her youthful charges and took a pull at The Saint. His blood was up, and he gave to her with the greatest reluctance, nearly pulling her arms from their sockets halfway down the steep incline as he went through the motions of cantering on the spot Fiona realised, with some amusement, that dressage movements were, after all, as their advocates claimed, based upon the natural movements of the horse. She had never been nearer to achieving a *piaffe* than she was at the moment.

Two of the pupils shot past her, completely out of control, followed by her employer in the same condition. Realising that it behoved her to keep an eye on the other three, Fiona turned The Saint around with difficulty and rode him up to the top of the hill again. A depressing sight, which promised effectively to scotch all chances of a hunt for her, met her eyes. Two of the Moorview horses had decided to turn nappy and the third was standing on his hind legs while his rider was apparently doing her best to pull him over backwards.

As Fiona collected the unhappy girls together and escorted them sedately down the hill, uttering instructions non-stop and hoping desperately that they would prove to be the right ones, she realised for the first time just how frustrating it can be to act as nursemaid to anyone in the hunting field. Once on the flat again, and with the young horses now moderately controllable, she led them away at a sedate trot in the direction which hounds seemed to have taken.

There were many worse ways of spending a morning than riding through the high-banked Devonshire lanes in the autumn sunshine, but it was hardly hunting. They jogged along for some fifteen minutes before they came upon the tail of the hunt, ploughing along in the same direction. It consisted of a very ancient retired Army officer, she guessed, mounted on an equally aged animal that was scarcely bigger than a pony, and escorting a small boy, probably his grandson, on a little grey donkey. He greeted her with a cheery nod.

"We're not the last, then, after all! Do you think they came this way?"

"I hope so!" replied Fiona.

"Funny sort of cub-hunting, this. I've brought my grandson out to stand around quietly and look at hounds, as I thought, and look what we've let ourselves in for!"

Fiona smiled and trotted on, followed by her silent retinue who were too busy riding to utter one word. The blood horse was pulling like a train, but otherwise he seemed to possess no idiosyncrasies. The young horses were settling gradually, and Fiona had ceased to worry that she would have to pick up a body from the road and find herself with an accident on her hands.

They passed through a copse where The Saint seemed to think he should canter and Fiona, weakly, let him. The others followed suit, and the little band was brought to an abrupt halt by a gate at the end of the ride. Beyond it lay a field which sloped steeply downwards and far below them in the valley she could at last see hounds.

Somehow or other they reached the bottom safely, though not without a few anxious moments with one of the youngsters insisting on making his descent sideways, like a crab. The Saint had a good pair of shoulders despite the length of his back, and they worked like pistons as he ate up the field with long, raking strides. He was, despite his appearance, all that could be desired as a comfortable ride, and Fiona recalled the old maxim immortalised by Snaffles in his print " 'Andsome is as 'andsome does."

They left the field by means of an open gate and trotted on through another wood. Ahead they could see a little knot of people gathered around something on the ground.

"Have they killed the fox?" asked one of her companions excitedly.

"It's hardly likely, when hounds are still running on ahead," replied Fiona tersely. It seemed far more likely to her that someone had had a bad fall, and this opinion was corroborated a moment later. A farmer came cantering towards her and asked:

"Are you the new young lady from the Moorview?" Fiona nodded in surprise.

"Then if I were you I'd take these lasses home. Mrs. Prendergast has had a nasty toss and they're taking her off to hospital. I'll bring her horse along later. The other two young ladies have already started back on their own."

Mrs. Prendergast had, in fact, broken her pelvis when the idiot chestnut mare had slipped up on the flat and fallen on her. Fiona's natural distress at the mishap was deepened to something very nearly akin to despair by the nagging realisation that now there was no question of giving the situation, as she had fondly imagined, a week's trial. There was, indeed, no prospect of escape for weeks or even months ahead, for how could she desert a sinking ship and leave all those horses to the tender mercies of a handful of inexperienced girls and a man who, delightful as he might be, would be completely hopeless as a guiding light for the *ménage?*

Her employer, when she visited her in the Exeter hospital the following day, looked tinier than ever as she lay in bed in a vast ward full of depressing female fracture cases. The fighting spirit seemed to have died in her, and she seemed somehow pathetic lying flat on her back in a voluminous, faded pink nightdress.

"Ridiculous thing to do," she said weakly by way of greeting. "How are you managing? I'm afraid there's a great deal to do with one pair of hands missing."

"Well, we've not done too badly so far. There haven't been any dramas, and the girls are really very good. Do you want me to take them out hunting again on Saturday?"

"Yes, I want to be able to sell those horses as made hunters as soon as possible, so the oftener they go out, the better. I think you'll find everything fairly plain sailing. If you need anything, tell my husband, I'm very thankful to have you to depend on, Fiona. I really don't know what I should have done without you at a time like this."

Feeling somewhat trapped, Fiona went back to

find a telegram from Gavin awaiting her. Lucifer had finished second in the regional final of the Foxhunter competition and had thereby qualified to jump for the championship at Wembley the following month. Fiona sat for some time with the telegram in her hands. Wellesley Hall and Gavin and Lucifer seemed somehow to be part of another life that had been lived centuries ago. Then she sat down and wrote a letter to congratulate Gavin, and to give him a graphic description of her new job and the plight in which she now found herself. The reply, when it arrived, offered little in the way of sympathy. It would do Fiona good to rough it for a while, she learned, and the experience of having so many responsibilities would be nothing but beneficial!

As the weeks went by she found that she was enjoying her authoritative position more than she had ever expected to. She had never worked so hard in her life, nor lived so ungraciously. The French and needlework courses that she had taken appeared to have been so much waste of time; but she did find time occasionally, the cooking also having fallen to her lot, to produce meals that had apparently never appeared on the oil-cloth while Mrs. Prendergast was in command of the kitchen range. There were eggs and there was cream in plenty, and she used both liberally and enthusiastically.

Gradually she came to enjoy the Devonshire

hunting more than she had ever expected to. She found a sporting cameraderie among these small fields that had been totally absent from the milling masses that turned out in Gloucestershire, and she already knew all the hunting people for miles around. She found a rusty old bit in the tack room which was actually capable of holding The Saint, and he carried her safely and well as she chaperoned her little herd. The young horses, too, were improving with each outing. By the end of the season they would all be able to carry a novice rider with a reasonable degree of safety, provided that he was not particularly ambitious about jumping fences. Fiona found that the in-country fences were virtually unjumpable, and that on the moor there were so many gaps in the stone walls that it was not easy to jump half a dozen obstacles during a day.

She felt a tremendous sense of responsibility towards the willing, overworked girls who were here to gain a certificate that would ensure employment for them in the career of their choice. None of them came from well-to-do families, and they depended tremendously upon passing the exam so that they might go out into the world and earn their own living. She taught them everything that she could, and felt a terrific sense of achievement when she noted improvement in one of them.

On one memorable October evening she went to a nearby farmer's house and watched the

Foxhunter championship being televised from the Horse of the Year show. When Gavin and Lucifer entered the ring—the horse looking so mature and sophisticated with his mane plaited and bandages on his forelegs—she tensed with anxiety, and her nails dug into the palms of her hands when he came wrong at the double and Gavin did nothing to put him right. Both elements fell, and Fiona expelled all the breath from her lungs in a sigh of disappointment. She was flattered, but hardly consoled, to receive Gavin's letter of confession that he had "ridden him like an idiot", and the admission that, had she but been on the horse's back, Lucifer would probably have won.

CHAPTER IX

Point-to-Point

"Fiona, how would you like to ride The Saint in a couple of point-to-points this Spring?" asked Mrs. Prendergast one morning early in January. She had returned from hospital but was still more or less bedridden. It was a crisp, frosty morning when the ground was so hard and slippery as to make hunting impossible. The freeze-up had lasted for nearly a week and the horses were all short of work and foolishly fresh in consequence.

"Why, I'd love it! I've never ridden in a race, though, and I really don't know the first thing about it."

"The horse will teach you all he knows, and so will I," promised her employer. "He was raced over banks in Ireland as a three-year-old, and as you know he's a very safe jumper over banks and flies. He's been well hunted, too—there would be no difficulty in getting a Master's certificate for him, for he's really qualified already."

"What does qualification actually imply? I'm a bit vague about it."

"Why, simply that he's been regularly and

fairly hunted—that is, he must have been out with hounds at least ten times during the current season, and kept out until two o'clock: not simply shown hounds and then taken home, as some of the point-to-point people would like to do if they could get away with it. No one could deny that The Saint's done his turn well and truly."

The prospect of riding The Saint in a few races made all the difference to Fiona's outlook on life. Now there was really something to look forward to and to work for, and though she would never feel about The Saint, much as she had come to like him, as she had about her first love, Lucifer, there was something about the ugly, iron-mouthed, courageous youngster that drew her to him. Now that her pupils were coming along so nicely and she was not required to hover about them all the time like an anxious hen she had had some great hunts on The Saint, and there is nothing like a shared experience—or rather, a series of them—for creating a bond of sympathy, whether it be with an animal or a human being.

Mrs. Prendergast had a farmer friend a few miles across the valley who trained a few point-to-pointers and hunter 'chasers privately, and he was only too willing to help with The Saint's preparation. Fiona rode over there several times for a school over the regulation fences he had put up around his farm, and he himself rode alongside her on a seasoned old horse that he kept as a schoolmaster for his own youngsters.

It was tremendously exhilarating, Fiona found, and she realised that for sheer excitement this form of riding left show jumping cold, but it was not easy at first to discard all of her show-jumping technique and adopt an entirely different style to that which she had practised for so long. Jumping fences at racing speed was a very different proposition from jumping them slowly in the knowledge that merely a flick would send a pole crashing to the ground, and she found it particularly difficult not to "place" The Saint at his fences, and to resist taking a pull as she rode into them. The knowledge of a horse's stride that she had acquired, however, did prove useful in this new *métier*, and it was something that she might never have learned without her experience over show-ring fences.

The Saint loved his work, for nothing pleased him better than to gallop and jump. Fiona had tremendous confidence in him by this time. Though he took a strong hold, she had learned to let him go on without fighting with him, and in so doing she had discovered that when she really wanted to stop him, she could. They had come to understand one another perfectly. Fiona had ceased to be haunted by visions of being run away with, while the horse knew now that no pain was to be inflicted upon his mouth.

At the end of January he was given his hunter's certificate and Fiona stopped hunting him. For the next six weeks, until the start of the point-to-point season started, his programme was to consist of getting racing fit, rather than hunting fit. For the horse who is in good condition for being five or six hours a day at comparatively slow paces is in no state to stay three miles and jump a dozen fences or so at racing pace.

His corn ration was increased until he was putting away twenty pounds a day with no difficulty at all, and simultaneously his hay allowance was reduced. His exercise consisted of hours and hours of walking and slow trotting up the steepest hills in the neighbourhood, with a half-speed canter every few days to open up his lungs and break the monotony. After exercise Fiona strapped him until her arms were aching, banging away at his back and quarters to build up the muscle. Gradually he became as fit as a fighting cock, and Mrs. Prendergast pronounced herself well satisfied with his preparation.

"It's a pity we can't run him in our hunt members' race—he'd walk away with it," she said. "As things are, you can only ride him in the ladies' race, which is the hottest and fastest race of the day at nearly every meeting. We should be living in Ireland—there all the races are open to women, and they can ride against the men as often as they please."

"Would The Saint stand a better chance of winning the members' race than the ladies'?" asked Fiona thoughtfully.

"Much better—there aren't many race horses in the hunt, as you know. The hunt race never takes a lot of winning down here, but it's confined to gentlemen riders."

Making a great effort, for she hated the thought of anyone else riding the horse on which she had worked so hard, Fiona said: "I wonder if Mr. Brimacombe would ride him for us? Then I could ride him in the ladies' races at the adjacent meetings."

"It's an idea. We'll ring him up and ask him. It's a gesture, too, after the number of times he's let us school over his fences."

Somewhat to Fiona's relief, however, Mr. Brimacombe was riding one of his own horses in the members' race. "I haven't a particularly strong team for this year, and I want to make sure of winning one race, anyway," he told them. "And don't be too sure that Fiona won't win the ladies' race on him. That's a useful horse you have there, and she rides him well. All she wants is a bit of experience between the flags, and she won't get that by standing in the paddock and watching me ride him."

So The Saint was duly entered for the ladies' race at the South Dartmoor Foxhounds' point-to-point, and the race-card named Miss F. Jamieson as his rider and "blue, with blue cap" as her colours.

A cattle truck arrived from the local market town on the morning of the races to take the horse, his jockey and the entire covey of working pupils to the course. Mr. and Mrs. Prendergast were to follow later in the ramshackle van, in which a makeshift bed of horse-blankets and pillows had been arranged to give Mrs. Prendergast, who planned to watch through the windows, as comfortable a grandstand as possible.

Fiona, secure in the knowledge that The Saint, at least, had been trained and produced to the minute, wished that she had as great a confidence in herself. She was feeling far worse than ever she had before a show jumping competition, for there was a certain amount of fear of physical danger in the back of her mind. She knew that racing was a far more hazardous pursuit than jumping show fences, and Mrs. Prendergast was a warning as to the pain and discomfort associated with broken bones. Try as she might to dismiss the thought, reproaching herself with arrant cowardice, she could not quite dispel the horrid expectation of being carried away on a stretcher, encased in a plaster cast and equipped with a pair of crutches.

The sight of The Saint emerging like a Grand National candidate from his box did a little, however, towards restoring her peace of mind. No craven fears for him, he seemed to say, as he strode down the ramp with his head held high and his ears pricked, looking around him and surveying the scene with unaffected delight. The working pupils buzzed around him like bees around their queen, removing his kneecaps and bandages, putting on his snaffle bridle with its blue and white browband. He looked every inch a racehorse, and Fiona only wished that she felt a little more like a jockey.

While his attendants, filled with self-importance, led him away to the paddock where horses were already parading, she made her way down the field to the secretary's tent to get her number and a racecard. The white cloth was printed with a large black "7", and she felt slightly better as she contemplated riding under her lucky number. Then she consulted the race-card. There were thirteen entries for the Ladies' Cup, if they all ran. If this were another omen, she hoped that they did not.

The dressing and weighing-in tents lay behind the paddock, and she went down there to deposit her handbag, saddle and boots before setting out to walk the course. When she came out she found Mr. Brimacombe waiting for her.

"Come on," he said, "I must spy out the lie of the land too. We might as well do it together."

He was so easy and relaxed that Fiona found herself relaxing too. They laboured along in their gum-boots and duffle coats across ploughed fields and grassland, climbing up on banks and jumping down again the other side, subjecting each fence to the minutest scrutiny. The course was absolutely straightforward, other than one drop fence on to good, sound turf, and the going was dry enough to prevent the take-offs and landings becoming poached. Conditions were ideal, and on this score at least she knew that she had no cause to worry.

She was glad to see her mentor on his white-faced, white-legged, rather peacocky chestnut gelding, winning the members' race by a distance, and she watched him very closely in the hope of profiting from his experience. He rode a waiting race, which would not be a very easy thing to do on The Saint, who even in his schooling gallops always liked to make the running. Just before the last fence he turned on the tap to overtake the two plodders who lay ahead of him, and he forged away on the flat to win as he liked.

Mr. Prendergast arrived just after this race and parked the van at the top of a hill, in order that his wife might have the best possible view of the racing. Fiona had packed the back of the van with thermos flasks of steaming black coffee and tins of sandwiches, and the girls arrived in relays to attack them. The Saint was being walked around quietly while the first two races took place, looking resplendent in a camel-coloured rug that had been unearthed from the mothballs the previous evening.

"I think you'd better go down to the dressing-tent and put your boots on," remarked Mrs. Prendergast at last. "Good luck, my dear. Keep out of trouble, and win if you can."

The dressing-tent was full of an assorted collection of ladies, both young and not-so-young, formidable and fearful. Apart from one little farmer's daughter who was gamely having a go on her hunting pony Fiona knew none of them, but a snatch of overheard conversation put her on her mettle.

"I know them all, I think, except the Moorview Stables' entry—a horse called The Saint. Nothing to fear there, I'm sure. You know what Mrs. Prendergast's horses are like—half-fit, and ridden by half-baked girls."

Fiona glanced up quickly from wrestling with her boot-hooks. The speaker was a tough-looking woman with a jutting jaw, heavily made-up and wearing a scarlet sweater and racing cap. She looked extremely proficient and as hard as nails, and her number was 13. Looking down at her card, Fiona discovered her to be none other than Lady Lovibond, a famous lady rider whose photograph was constantly appearing in the pages of the glossy magazines.

When she had weighed-out and filled her weight-cloth with the appropriate amount of lead, Fiona carried her saddle out to the paddock, where The Saint was being led round by one of his faithful attendants. Mr. Brimacombe appeared to help with the saddling operations, and with his number cloth and his blue and white surcingle in place The Saint really looked the part. Fiona jumped into the plate with a confidence she was far from feeling and followed old Tom Firkin, who had apparently borrowed a really red coat for the occasion, down to the start.

They lined up without any trouble, though Lady Lovibond's raking grey gelding kept swinging his quarters around ominously, and at last the starter dropped his flag. Then they were away towards the first fence in a cavalry charge, already fighting for a place although there was so far to go.

Fiona let The Saint go on at his own speed, merely steadying him a little going into the first. He jumped it beautifully, and then, much to his rider's surprise, settled down and hardly pulled at all. He was running his own race and she was little more than a passenger, she knew, but when he jumped the second fence as well as he had the first with no directions from her, she knew that the best tactics would be to sit still and leave him alone as much as possible. He seemed perfectly happy striding along at the head of the second division, and he was well in touch with the leaders.

Lady Lovibond, who prided herself on her dash, was making the running. Behind her lay two determined-looking younger women, and then, neck and neck, lay the farmer's daughter and Fiona. The former's half-bred pony was running on very gallantly, but Fiona knew that he could never stay three miles at this sort of pace, and that soon he must shoot his bolt. Behind her was the steady thud of galloping hooves on the turf and some half-dozen riders, all content to bide their time.

The order remained virtually unchanged until the drop fence, where drama overtook them. One of the horses ahead of her jumped crookedly across it, interfering with the other and bringing it down. In mid-air Fiona was desperately fearful of landing in the thick of the melee, but somehow The Saint managed to avoid the fallen horse and his prostrate rider. As he landed he pecked slightly, but after a magnificent recovery he found his stride again and was galloping on in pursuit of the others.

"I must avoid that bay horse at all costs," Fiona told herself. She knew that what had happened to the other horse and rider could just as well happen to her if she jumped abreast of him or too soon after. Reluctant as she was to interfere with The Saint or put any pressure on him so early, she nevertheless urged him on before the next fence loomed ahead. He responded willingly enough, and surged past the bay horse to fall into place behind the bobbing red cap.

They jumped three more fences thus, with Fiona lying second. Occasionally she glanced backwards over her shoulder, unable to control an irresistible impulse to see how closely the others were following. The field was by now well spread-out, but there were two or three riders, their faces grimly determined, pursuing her fairly closely and she knew that she was by no means certain of a place, even with the race more than half run.

Now they were jumping on to plough, and the heavier going immediately slowed them up. The Saint was going better, however, than the grey horse, and slowly but inexorably he began to gain on it. Now it was the turn of the red cap to glance backwards over her shoulder, but she was too experienced a jockey to risk more than a swift look.

Two more plain fences lay ahead of them before a right-handed turn around a flag would lead them into the straight run to the judges' wagon and the winning post. Once round the flag, Fiona determined to make her effort. She squeezed The Saint with her legs, and immediately he quickened and lengthened his stride. He was still full of running, and the grey horse appeared to be almost standing still as he ate up the distance between them.

They jumped the last fence neck and neck and The Saint, who was the better jumper, gained half-a-length as they landed. The rider in red had got her whip out and was feinting with it laboriously, but Fiona's horse needed no urging. He lengthened his lead as Fiona shifted her position further forward, and as they galloped up the straight she heard the roars of the crowd who were thronging the ropes. Then the judges' wagon shot past and she knew that she had won.

"By Jove, that horse is fit!" she heard a man's voice declaiming as she pulled up. "Look at him —he could go round again!"

"He's got a bit more class than Mrs. Prendergast's usual animals, hasn't he?" came the reply. "Still, I suppose by the law of averages everyone must get hold of a good 'un now and again. Not a bad jockey, either. The place must be looking up a bit."

As she rode back to the paddock to weigh in, surrounded by a bevy of excited pupils who were all trying to pat The Saint at once and nearly coming to blows for the honour of leading him in, Mr. Prendergast came tearing up, flushed with emotion.

"Oh, that was wonderful, Fiona!" he gasped. "Well done, indeed! My wife is thrilled to bits— it's done her all the good in the world! Come up to the van and see her as soon as you've weighed in. I'm going to buy a bottle of champagne!"

Mr. Brimacombe was waiting by the winners' enclosure to add his congratulations, and all the friends she had made out hunting patted her on the back as she took off The Saint's saddle and made her way to the scales. Then she went back to see that the horse was rugged up properly before he was led away to the lorry. His veins were standing out all over his body, his coat was dark with sweat and his nostrils were so distended that they were twice their normal size, but he was quite undistressed by his exertions. Patting his heaving, dripping flank, Fiona felt a rush of gratitude towards him.

"We won't keep him hanging about here,'" she said to the driver. "I'll be back in a minute, and we'll take him on home and give him a good mash. You girls put his bandages on and load him up. Let him have a small drink, but don't overdo it or he may get a chill, or even colic."

She collected her things from the dressing tent and made her way back to the car. Mrs. Prendergast lay jubilant upon her pillows. She stretched out her hand and clasped Fiona's in a vice-like grip.

"Well done, my dear. You rode him beautifully—it's a great achievement to win one's very first race, you know. And in such distinguished company. That grey horse of Lady Lovibond's was almost unbeaten last season."

"The Saint is a very good horse," said Fiona. "He did it all, really. All I had to do was to sit there and leave it to him."

"Yes, he's even better than I thought he was. One of my luckier buys. I must send a telegram to his breeder in Tipperary to-night—he'll be overjoyed that the horse has turned out so well. I daresay I can make a good price of him now—thanks very largely to you. But I won't sell him until the end of the season, unless I get an exceptional offer. You shall have your fun on him after all the hard work you've put in."

The spring passed quickly enough after that. The Saint had three more races, two of which he won, and on the third occasion he finished an honourable second to a former 'chaser from up-country who had been unbeaten during three seasons and later won the Foxhunters' at Liverpool. But he never fell or even made a bad mistake, and, as Mr. Brimacombe pointed out, he was worth a thousand pounds of anybody's money.

Gradually Mrs. Prendergast started to get about, and Fiona began to wonder when she could decently broach the question of leaving. She had adapted herself to the Moorview Riding School by now, and she had almost enjoyed quite a lot of her stay there, but the time had come to find a more congenial position with better living conditions. She wanted, too, to get back in the show ring again, and though The Saint had turned out to be a good racehorse in disguise there was nothing in the stable that bore the slightest resemblance to a show jumper.

She felt a certain responsibility, however, to the working pupils, as well as to her employer, and she determined to stay until they had taken their

B.H.S. exams. They were enthusiastic and conscientious and pathetically eager to learn, and with any luck they would all pass and obtain certificates.

One day she told Mrs. Prendergast of her decision.

"I was afraid of that," she replied, after a brief pause. "It's good of you to have stayed as long as you have. We should have been in a sorry state without you this winter. When do you want to go?"

"At the end of April, I think," said Fiona. "I should like a show jumping job for the summer, anyway. Afterwards, I'll see what turns up."

"Well, you know you can come back here any time you like. There will always be a place for you if you care to come. In the meantime, you had better put an advertisement in the paper. Show jumping jobs get snapped up early, and you don't want to miss the boat."

"Who will you get in my place?" asked Fiona, curiously.

"I hadn't thought—I might even keep on one of our own girls when she's passed her exam. Christine's improved enormously since you've been here—I might ask her if she'd be interested. What do you think?"

"I think she'd be very good. She's hard-working and she loves it here." Nor, thought Fiona to herself, does she want very much from life. A handful of horses to look after and ride, and Christine would be happy almost anywhere.

In April, life became more hectic than ever, for mares were arriving almost daily to visit one or other of the stallions, in addition to the normal work, that went on about the place and the cramming the girls required for their exams. At the same time Fiona's advertisement appeared in *Horse and Hound*, and replies seemed to come in by every post. Few of them appealed to her particularly, for most appeared to require girl grooms rather than riders, but Fiona was nothing if not conscientious and she sat up in bed night after night burning the midnight oil and answering them laboriously.

Then, in the midst of it all, the unexpected happened. One morning at breakfast a telegram arrived. It said: DEIDRE LEAVING TO GET MARRIED WOULD YOU LIKE HER JOB and it was signed ANSTRUTHER.

Fiona's reply was equally brief and to the point. It simply said YES.

CHAPTER X

Lucifer Again

Fiona could hardly believe her good luck as she sat on the platform at Bristol Temple Meads station, awaiting her connection to Meltonham. She had been so delighted at the prospect of returning to the place where she had been so happy that she had elected to come straight up from Devonshire to take up her new position. Mrs. Prendergast, who was not given to expressing any form of emotion, had been touchingly sorry to see her go. She had presented her with a large tin of Devonshire cream and a framed photograph of herself on The Saint, taken in the paddock after a race, which Fiona treasured greatly.

The prospect of seeing the Anstruthers again was exciting, but best of all was the anticipation of a re-union with Lucifer and the knowledge that she would be able to ride him in the ring again. She wondered who in the world had decided that Deidre was his romantic ideal, and blessed him for his decision that had had such far-reaching, beatific repercussions. Maybe it was the hunting farmer who had been partly responsible for

Lindsay's premature departure from Wellesley Hall. If so, Deidre would probably insist upon teaching him dressage and supervising the schooling of his long-suffering show jumpers. Then would the repercussions be far-reaching indeed!

At last her train arrived to take her on the last stage of the journey, and as it chugged up through the Gloucestershire countryside until they were in the Cotswolds again, with its neat stone walls, enormous flat fields and towering trees—so different from the tiny, patchwork-quilt Devonshire countryside, scattered with stunted oaks—Fiona mused on the first time she had arrived at Wellesley Hall. Then, only just over eighteen months before, she had been the greenest pupil it was possible to find, hero-worshipping the horse but knowing next to nothing about him. Now, rich in experience, with her chosen career in its proper perspective, she was returning to pass on that experience to others, now as raw as she had once been. She marvelled to herself at the change in her circumstances.

Instead of Colonel Anstruther, this time Gavin was on the platform to meet her. He shook her warmly by the hand and picked up her bags.

"It's good to see you again, Fiona," he greeted her. "We all missed you when you left."

He led the way out of the station to the waiting Land-Rover. The old lurcher, Fly, was lying in the back, just as he had been on the occasion of

Fiona's first arrival. She spoke to him and stroked his head as she climbed into the front seat, and he thumped his tail on the steel floor in response.

"He hasn't forgotten you," Gavin remarked. "He's paying you a great compliment, you know. His tail only wags for the people he considers worthy of his notice, and they're few and far between!"

On the way to Wellesley Hall he asked her all sorts of questions about her life in Devonshire, and seemed interested in her account of the point-to-points.

"You did a good job, running the whole show on your own like that," he said. "I told you the responsibility would do you good, didn't I? You've grow up since you left us."

"And how is Lucifer?" asked Fiona. "I'm longing to see him again."

"He's in excellent form, and I don't think I've done him any harm!" laughed Gavin. "You can give me your verdict when you ride him tomorrow. He's a bit of a one-man horse, though, you know. He never went for me as he used to for you. Once we put Deidre on him to see if he simply preferred a lady on his back, but she couldn't get on with him at all, so I've always ridden him ever since. We'll have to have a crack at some of the bigger shows this year. He's upgraded himself now, and he jumps even better over the higher fences than he did over novice courses. My father thinks the sun rises and sets for him."

The familiar and beautiful old Cotswold-stone house looked welcoming as they turned in through the gates, and there were still young horses, covered with mud, in the field where she had first set eyes on Lucifer. Gavin drove up to the front door and stopped with a flourish, and a couple of young fox-hounds came gambolling down the steps to meet them.

"A couple of hound puppies we've got at walk," Gavin explained. "They're a menace—chew anything within sight and spend the rest of their time chasing the fowls. We'll have an interesting season when they are entered! Come in and see Mother. She's longing to see you again."

Mrs. Anstruther, still followed by her trio of whippets, came half-way to the door to greet her.

"Bless you, Fiona dear," she said, bestowing a kiss on her cheek. "How lovely it is to see you again—come in and have a glass of sherry before you go upstairs, and tell me all about what you've been doing. It seems that you have turned into a highly efficient and responsible young woman, just as I had always imagined that you would!"

She listened with interest, and sometimes with amusement, to Fiona's description of the establishment in which she had been working for the last eight months.

"It all sounds a little unorthodox, but it's just

the course that I should have recommended for you to widen your experience," she remarked, stroking the oldest whippet who lay curled up in her lap. "You know, when you had finished your time with us I was very sorely tempted to ask you to remain. But I knew that you must go away and accept some responsibility before you were ready to take your place here. It's all turned out even better than I had hoped, and I couldn't be more pleased about it. I hope that you will stay with us for many years. Now, my dear, you must be longing for a bath after all that time on the train. I will take you up to your room, and you must dine with us at our table to-night."

It seemed strange to find herself in a pretty little room at the family's end of the house, and stranger still to see the dining room full of new faces. Only Mam'selle was familiar.

"*Eh bien, ma chère!*" she greeted her affectionately, bestowing a light kiss on each cheek. "*Je suis heureux de vous voir. Comment allez-vous?*"

"*Très bien, merci,*" replied Fiona with an effort, marvelling at the speed with which her French had deserted her during her sojourn in Devonshire.

The pupils looked incredibly young, rather to her relief. They were, nevertheless, far more sophisticated than Mrs. Prendergast's working pupils, and the prospect of instructing them was still a little frightening. One, she knew, had already made a name for herself in Pony Club One-day events. The daughter of a rich Midlands industrialist, she had been given expensive, highly-trained ponies from the time that she could ride without a leading rein, and she was generally rather pleased with herself. Fiona knew that she would have to be on her mettle to achieve the necessary pupil-teacher relationship, and she hoped that she would be capable of doing so. As if reading her thoughts, Mrs. Anstruther remarked, while they were drinking their soup:

"Of course, Fiona, you are really very young to instruct here, but we all have every confidence in your ability, and you must have confidence too."

"Yes, don't let them rattle you," put in Gavin. "There's nothing they like better if you give them half a chance. You must develop a forbidding manner so that they will know better than to take any liberties with you!"

"There's no need to go to those lengths!" remonstrated the Colonel. "Heaven preserve me from a forbidding female! What a horrible prospect! By the way, Fiona, we thought we'd take Lucifer to have a crack at Badminton this year? Are you game?"

"In the Three-Day Event?" gasped Fiona in astonishment.

"No, no—in the jumping competitions that are held in conjunction with it. We must see about training an event horse for next year, but Lucifer can stick to show jumping. He's too good a jumper to confine him to small fences all his life, however difficult they may be. And they're too damned difficult sometimes, to my way of thinking. Laming and maiming good horses is not my idea of horsemanship."

"It's rather like the Grand National," said Mrs. Anstruther. "Unless they run into bad luck and get brought down or hampered by a loose horse, the good horses can get around Aintree without hurting themselves. It's the not-so-good horses that cause the trouble. Some of the foreign horses in competitions are inadequately trained and ridden and a few aren't even fit. If their owners had been a little wiser they would not even have been entered."

"It's a fascinating sport, for all that," said Gavin. "I intend to get a combined-training horse for next year—I may put that new grey Irish horse in for a few combined training competitions this summer. Show jumping is all very well, but there's too strong a professional element for my liking. The other game's a lot cleaner and more sporting. With all of these enormous money prizes being offered for show jumping it's got too jolly serious—a lot of the fun's gone out of it now."

"Don't forget that you are virtually a professional, will you?" laughed his father. "I suppose we can get around that somehow and get you and Fiona amateur licences—other people seem to manage it all right—but it's hardly adhering to the letter of the law."

"Nowadays it doesn't much matter," Gavin replied. "The line between amateurs and professionals is very finely drawn. I shouldn't be surprised to see them doing away with the distinction before very long."

"Look at some of the people who are going abroad with the team to-day," put in Fiona. "Most of them rely entirely on show jumping for their livelihood, but they've all got amateur licences. I suppose they have a few acres and they call themselves farmers."

"I know one who calls himself a journalist!" said Mrs. Anstruther. "Yet he only writes about show jumping and he never does anything else. If you know the right people, the powers-that-be turn a blind eye. They'd be silly not to, if they want to send the best riders abroad."

"Imagine being asked to jump for Britain!" mused Fiona dreamily. "It's my greatest ambition."

"Well, it just could happen to you if Lucifer turns out to be all that we hope," said the Colonel encouragingly. "If he goes well during the early part of the summer we might take him up to Wembley in July for the International Horse Show. He should be a good advertisement for us, even if he doesn't win the Queen Elizabeth Cup—which is rather a lot to expect of a horse who started last season as novice!"

Fiona soon got accustomed to her new position of authority, and she enjoyed instructing the girls in the school where she had once been through the mill. But most of all she enjoyed being reunited with Lucifer. The bay gelding was patently delighted to see her when first she visited him in his box, and he leaned his head against her fondly while she played with his ears.

"You and I are going to do great things together, old man—at least, I hope we are," she told him softly. "I can hardly wait to take you to a show again."

She did not have long to wait, for the days sped by and almost before she knew it Badminton loomed ahead of her. As she and Gavin drove through the wrought-iron gates at the main entrance, with the splendid old house on their right, the Royal standard fluttering in the breeze before and above it, she knew that this was her most thrilling experience of all. There were thousands of people milling hither and yon through the wide, rolling expanses of Badminton Park with its beautiful grassland and its age-old trees, and somewhere among them, speeding from fence to fence in a Land-Rover, was the Queen and the rest of the Royal Family.

Directly ahead of them lay the enormous main ring, flanked by the grandstand and an open stand opposite it. Surrounding the arena and its environs was a veritable village of shining white tents—the avenues of trade stands, selling everything from saddles and horse trailers to sporting prints, and the colossal luncheon marquees.

On their way to the horse-box park they passed row upon row of cars, with their roofs sparkling in the sunshine. Then there was another big jumping ring in which a competition was already taking place, and finally they came to the horse-boxes—literally hundreds of them.

"Getting cold feet?" grinned Gavin, with a sideways glance at her.

"I've got them already! Do you suppose I shall fall off in front of the Queen?"

"You've got a fifty-fifty chance of doing so—but then, so has everyone else. I shouldn't let it worry you unduly!"

Lucifer was by now in grade B, the intermediate classification. The fences, though not as big as the grade A horses have to tackle, were still much more imposing than those of the Foxhunter courses to which Fiona was accustomed. The competition, too, was stiffer than that in the novice events, for all of Lucifer's new collection of opponents had won more than £100 in prize money, which presupposed a certain amount of talent or an inordinate amount of luck.

While Fiona and one of the girls were unloading the horse and getting him ready Gavin wandered off in search of a programme. There was a constant stream of riders flowing past, warming up their horses and settling them down, and Lucifer, snatching at mouthfuls of grass whenever he succeeded in getting his head down, surveyed them with a cool detachment that Fiona was far from feeling. It was just as well, she thought, that one member of the partnership should be calm and collected. Just beyond them a tetchy thoroughbred mare was putting up a ridiculous performance while her attendants were endeavouring to get her saddled up, dancing around at the end of a lunge while they played her like a fish.

Badminton Park was a wonderful place to exercise. She cantered slowly away into the horizon, having first ascertained that she would not be trespassing on the cross-country course, and it seemed as though she could go straight on indefinitely with never a fence or a wall. On her way back she passed some of the fences that the Three-Day event horses, now engaged upon their dressage tests, would be jumping to-morrow. They looked as though they would be enormous fun to tackle, imposing though they were. Their solidity struck her most forcibly, and with it the full realisation that they were not to be trifled with.

When she got back Gavin was waiting for her.

"You're the first to jump, and they're starting in fifteen minutes," he said. "We've just got time to walk the course and get you organised. All the world and his wife are here. There are over forty in your section, and as many in two other sections. They'll be jumping the final at midnight, or thereabouts."

An excited pupil, trembling with self-importance, took Lucifer away to walk him around while Gavin and Fiona went through the collecting ring and into the arena to join the little band of black-capped, black-coated riders who were already inspecting the fences and pacing out the distances between them. Several were known to both of them by sight, and soon they were absorbed into the group—swelling now, as the time for the competition approached, and entirely preoccupied with the problem of the best place to take-off and the number of strides to take in the combinations. In addition to a double, there was also a treble fence, which Fiona had never before encountered. It was perfectly straight-forward, but it required concentration, with two non-jumping strides between its first two elements and three between the second and third.

The gate worried Fiona most of all, for it lay beyond a fairly sharp turn, and Lucifer was not yet sufficiently experienced to jump it at an angle. If she did not jump it squarely it was almost certain to fall, for it was supported somewhat precariously.

"That won't stand much clouting," remarked Gavin.

"No, it's the bogy, all right," agreed one of the professionals. "It'll sort us out a bit, I shouldn't be surprised."

"You'd never find a fence like this abroad," remarked a well-known international rider. "It doesn't encourage bold horses or bold riding at all. Some of our courses are ten years behind the times, but nobody seems to realise it. Dashed silly thing, in the middle of a galloping course, having to hook a horse back to jump it."

Fiona kept silent, but none of the foregoing was exactly calculated to instil her with confidence.

Back in the collecting ring she sprang lightly on to Lucifer's back and pressed him into a canter.

"You've just got time to give him a pop over the practice fence," called Gavin. "Then you can go straight in."

She was just touching down when her number was called, and she rode back into the collecting ring and out into the arena. A preliminary circle, and the bell went. She cantered through the start and set off on her round.

Lucifer jumped the first six fences like clockwork, and then the treble loomed ahead. The distances were dead right, and he went into and out of it beautifully, then on to a triple bar, well banked-up with brush, over which he flew. Then followed the right-angled turn, and the formidable gate was ready to present its challenge. Over-anxious, Fiona asked him off far too early, after checking him abruptly, but Lucifer was equal to the exigences of the occasion. He stood back and jumped off his hocks, landing safely the other side without a touch. Fiona's nervousness left her, and she rode him at the last three fences as though they were two foot high.

"Well, that's a good beginning!" Gavin was grinning broadly, plainly exultant. "There won't be too many clear rounds, I shouldn't think." Nor were there. Only five survived to contest the jump-off, and soon only two remained. One was Lucifer, the other a wiry little red-roan horse with scars on the front of his hocks, the mount of a professional from the North.

"Now you're against the clock," Gavin reminded her. "Don't go crazy and think it's a point-to-point you're riding, and don't take that gate too fast or you've had it."

As she went back into the ring again Fiona was beset by misgivings. She had negotiated the gate successfully twice, but would her luck hold for a third time? It seemed unlikely.

Afterwards she was at a loss to understand how it had happened. Lucifer was wrong going into the gate, and she tried to correct his stride. Too late, when he was almost underneath it, she asked him to take off, and for the first time ever he failed to comply. Instead, he ran out sideways at the very last moment, and Fiona, who had expected nothing of the kind, slid off over his shoulder, banging her own on the upright. She was physically unhurt, but her sensibilities were mortally wounded as she scrambled to her feet and made her way back to the collecting ring, where someone had retrieved Lucifer and was holding him for her to mount. She took him back and he jumped it perfectly amid applause from the grandstand, and finished the course without fault.

"It wasn't his fault, was it?" she asked Gavin anxiously. "He's never refused in his life!"

"No, it wasn't his fault, and it's nothing to worry about. A bit more experience for both of you will soon put things right."

"That's a good horse, and a clever one," put in one of the professionals who was standing beside them. "I'd sooner a horse ran out when he was wrong, any day, than one that'd bash through the lot and knock himself to bits attempting the impossible. He knew he couldn't make it, and he did the best he could. You don't want to hold that against him."

"If you want to part with him, I'll give you a fair price for him," offered another. "That's the time to buy, when they've made a mess of things! Would you take £500?"

"That wouldn't buy one leg!" laughed Gavin.

"Anyway, he's not for sale. There's another class for him to-morrow morning, and he's going to win that one!"

"Don't tempt providence!" said Fiona cautiously as they walked away.

"No, but I have a feeling, somehow. You all right?"

"Never better, but I feel like kicking myself. What did the roan horse do?"

"He had the gate down, and as he had all the time in the world he won as he liked. Never mind, we'll have his scalp to-morrow."

And, strangely enough, they did. When the box arrived back at Wellesley Hall there was a red rosette dangling from the windscreen. And it was no ordinary, common-or-garden ribbon, for it had been affixed to Lucifer's bridle by Royalty.

CHAPTER XI

Wembley

"Nothing succeeds like success!" quoted the Colonel rather tritely some weeks later, when Lucifer emerged from the main ring at the big Bath and West show after his biggest success to date. He and Fiona had just achieved a third clear round to win the Association's Grade B Championship, and Fiona was considerably elated. Already there was a string of rosettes, a fair percentage of them red ones, dangling gaily from the windscreen of the horse-box. Gavin declared it vulgar, but he made no move to take them down.

"Now he's upgraded himself, and he'll have to take on the grade A horses," said Fiona apprehensively. Her victory at Badminton had given her the confidence she needed, and by now her photograph had been plastered all over the local press, acclaiming her as a budding Ann Moore, while Lucifer was seen as a Foxhunter in the making: but none of this had gone to her head, and she was still uncertain as to her ability to make much of a showing against the established stars.

"He could have done with a little longer in Grade B, but we can't hold him back. We know that he jumps big fences better than he does small ones, anyhow," said the Colonel reassuringly. "He's inclined to be a bit careless over anything that he does not consider to be worthy of serious attention."

"We can't expect to have him winning Grade A competitions right away, but he'll soon find himself," added Gavin. "We'll get him going at the smaller shows—and we'll put him in a couple of classes at Wembley, too, just for fun. It's not until the end of July so we've got nearly six weeks ahead of us, and I don't think the entries are closed yet."

The following week, determined to give Lucifer as much experience as they could before taking him to London, they entered him at a small agricultural show near Badminton. It was an appalling day, with rain falling in sheets, and the going deteriorated rapidly into a quagmire. By the time the open jumping was scheduled to take place at the end of the afternoon the take-offs and landings were deep and poached, and the going on the flat was pretty slippery.

They screwed studs into Lucifer's shoes to give him a better purchase, and then Fiona rode him about in the mud churned up by the cattle lorries. The rain was running in streams off her hunting cap, and finding its way down her neck despite the fact that she had turned up her coat collar. Her lower arms and her thighs and knees were rapidly encased in thick, sodden garments, and she began to regret the mackintosh she had left behind. She could not have worn it in the ring, but it would at least have kept her dry throughout the preliminaries.

Before her turn came to enter the ring, Gavin said: "Now, take it easy to-day and don't risk giving Lucifer a fall. We don't want to undermine his confidence if we can help it. Go round nice and steadily and don't bother about time. Your point-to-pointing has given you a lot of drive and dash, which is all to the good, but it's better to forget them in going like this."

Fiona nodded and set off with extreme caution.

Lucifer was apparently determined to take care of himself too, and they jumped the first few fences out of the mud in a slow canter. Then, going into a fairly big spread, the worst happened. Lucifer slipped as he was taking off, and nearly fell over the fence, which he took by the roots. Miraculously he recovered his balance and landed intact the other side, but as he floundered to a slithering halt Fiona realised that all was not well and slipped off his back. Blood was already beginning to ooze from a deepish-looking cut on the back of his off-fore pastern, and with a sickening certainty she knew that he had over-reached himself.

"Well, that's that," said Gavin grimly, straightening up after examining the over-reach in the collecting ring. "It can't be helped and it wasn't your fault, Fiona—just thoroughly bad luck. If anyone's to blame it's I, for not putting over-reach boots on him. We shall just have to hope that it won't be a very long job and that he'll be fit for Wembley."

Keeping him fit was a difficult job, for his corn ration had to be cut drastically to keep his blood cool and prevent infection from setting up in the wound. There followed many anxious days, with Fiona leading him out for exercise every morning, before the veterinary surgeon finally pronounced him fit for work.

"We've lost a lot of valuable time, but we must just keep our fingers crossed," remarked the Colonel on the first day that Fiona was allowed to ride him again. "If he isn't going to do himself justice in London we won't take him there, that's all. There's always another year."

It was touch and go until a fortnight or so before the show started as to whether they would be able to take him, but at last they made up their minds to take the risk. His lack of experience of big shows was the greatest single factor militating against him, but he went well on his last outing before the journey and, as Gavin remarked, "Anything can happen in this game. I've seen a novice horse winning a championship at an international show."

The journey to London was undertaken on a scorching late-July day when the holiday traffic was reaching its peak. The cab of the horse-box was sweltering hot, and Fiona and Gavin sat in their shirt-sleeves, stopping frequently for ice-creams and fervently wishing that they had made a start earlier in the day.

The Anstuthers had decided to make the International Horse Show the occasion of their annual holiday, and they were taking the car up to London and staying at the pleasant, old-fashioned Knightsbridge hotel that is a home-from-home for hundreds of country people. They had booked a room there for Fiona too, but Gavin had elected to sleep at Wembley in order to keep an eye on the horse, and a camp bed with other essential requisites for a modicum of comfort had been stowed away in the back of the horse-box.

When they arrived at Wembley at tea-time the stables were a veritable hive of activity. Horse-boxes and Land-Rover-driven trailers were arriving almost every five minutes and the stable manager and his assistants, a burly contingent from the R.A.S.C., were having their work cut out to allocate loose boxes and deal with inquiries and requests in the little wooden hut that did duty as an office.

They were thrilled to find that Lucifer had been put in a line with the horses belonging to some of the foreign teams. On one side of him were the big, quality thoroughbreds of the American riders, and opposite were the heavier Holsteins and Hanoverians who were jumping for Germany. Next to the German horses stood the Spanish Army's representatives, attended by swarthy, black-haired grooms. Then came the big, heavy-weight-hunter-type Irish-bred animals with which the Italians intended to take the field.

Lucifer seemed quite unmoved by all the excitement as they took him out of the lorry and led him into the wooden box which was to be his home for the week. Fiona was a little disappointed to find that he took no more notice of his glamorous neighbours than he did of the horses that he jumped against each week at the country shows. She decided that he had no sense of occasion.

She herself was brimming over with excitement and even Gavin, once he had seen the horse settled down and feeding comfortably, was more disposed to wander about the stables, scrutinising the foreign horses and engaging their grooms in halting conversations, than he was to join his parents at their hotel for a bath and a meal.

They spent a lyrical couple of hours before, reluctantly, they crossed the road to the Underground station. That night at dinner everyone was in a festive mood.

"This takes me back to the old days at Olympia before the war," reminisced the Colonel. "That was a real International horse show. Everyone dressed in the evening, the place was a mass of flowers—Wembley will never be the same. It can't possibly be, in a place like that. No atmosphere, in comparison. Why, there's no room to exercise there, to begin with."

"Yet there *is* an atmosphere on the big nights," Mrs. Anstruther replied. "It's still the International, the one and only, after all. The young, who never knew Olympia, still think it's a wonderful week."

"I wonder how Lucifer will go under floodlights?" mused Gavin. "At any rate he'll have a chance to get accustomed to the arena to-morrow morning. I hope the courses are reasonable. Last year they were so twisty that no one could ride at them—hook, hook, hook all the time, yet they tell us they are trying to encourage horses to gallop on and jump freely."

"Fiona should go to bed early to-night," remarked Mrs. Anstuther. "It will be her only chance of an early night. We never seem to get back here before midnight once the show has started. We'll have breakfast at eight and then go straight to Wembley."

Fiona, however, slept badly that night. The

room was hot and stuffy, even with the window flung wide, and the constant hum and throb of the London traffic made sleep almost impossible for one who habitually dropped off to a silence only broken by the occasional hoot of an owl. The auspicious reason for her presence here, too, made her over-anxious and set up a nervous tension that kept her awake into the small hours. At length she fell asleep from sheer exhaustion to awake a few hours later feeling utterly unrested.

When they arrived at Wembley and made their way to the stables Gavin had already taken Lucifer out for his exercise.

"There's absolutely no room here to work a horse," he complained. "To-morrow morning I think I'll put him in the horse-box and take him to Hyde Park. A spin in the Row might amuse him and it'll do more good than anything I can give him here."

"Now darling, we'll take over while you get some breakfast," said his mother. "The competition doesn't start for nearly an hour so you've got plenty of time."

"Actually I've had breakfast—I had it with the grooms at six o'clock, thanks all the same," said Gavin with some pride. "Very good it was, too, and it cost next to nothing. I made friends with a German fellow, a very good chap and a real horseman. He told me several things about show jumping that I didn't know."

"I don't doubt that for a moment!" laughed his father.

"Some of the foreigners don't seem to be too fussy about what they do to their horses to make them jump," Gavin went on. "If I couldn't win competitions without that sort of thing I'd leave show jumping severely alone."

"Some of our own people couldn't learn much in that direction," said Mrs. Anstruther. "We ought to put our own house in order before we start to criticise the foreigners."

"We also ought to organise ourselves for the Welcome Stakes," said Gavin. "Come on, Fiona, all the hard work's been done! Now all you have to do is to go in and win!"

Fiona grimaced at him and patted Lucifer. "I wish I could, for his sake. Dear boy, he does try so hard to jump clear rounds. I'm quite sure that he knows when he's achieved one."

With Gavin walking beside her and his parents following in their wake she rode out through the gate on to the road and up past the officials' car park to the outer collecting ring. A practice jump had been put up here, and there was a steady stream of horses jumping backwards and forwards over it. None of the foreign riders was among them for this opening event was a national competition confined to British riders. Inwardly she fancied her chances in it less than in the ladies' competition the following evening, for she had all the professionals ranged against her and she knew only too well by now just how formidable they could be.

Her chief bugbear, she knew, would be the water jump, to which both she and Lucifer were comparatively new. They had practised jumping water at home and the horse, who had tremendous scope, made nothing of it, but Fiona had not yet quite mastered the not-inconsiderable art of riding at it either to her own or Gavin's complete satisfaction. Either she went too fast from too far away, in which case she brought him to the take-off unbalanced, or else she left it too late to turn on the tap sufficiently so that he had not enough impulsion to get him over and landed short.

On this occasion she was doomed to make the former mistake. Turning the corner at the top of the ring, she set off lickety-split. Lucifer cleared the spread of the water well enough, but as he had galloped right through the little hedge that was planted inconspicuously in front of it she left the ring to the tune of four faults. As there were already more clear rounds than there were prizes it put them right out of the hunt, and a disconsolate Fiona set off back to the stable.

"Cheer up," said Gavin consolingly. "It's not a bad beginning. You jumped a clear round, you know, except for the water, which is pretty good for a first attempt. Besides, I have good news for you. I've just seen the plan of the course for to-morrow night and there's no open water in it at all; simply a biggish parallels with water underneath that you can treat as though it isn't there."

For the rest of the day they had a holiday watching the hunters and the hackneys and, in the evening session, the thrilling Welcome Parade of the foreign teams, led by the mounted band of the Life Guards with the four State Trumpeters on their grey horses and the big skewbald drum horse, Hannibal, majestically leading the colourful procession. Behind the black troop horses each of the teams was headed by a Hussar, bearing aloft its national flag, and the Queen was in the Royal Box to take the salute.

"It makes me feel shivery with excitement," Fiona confided to Gavin as they stood together leaning over the white rails in an unaccustomed holiday mood. Fiona, for once not in jodhpurs, breeches or boots, had put on a cotton dress and Gavin, who looked very handsome in a dark grey suit, smiled down at her approvingly with an unwontedly soft expression in his clear grey eyes. Fiona smiled back, suddenly strangely shy, and felt a new and inexplicable bond between them. She thought back fleetingly to her previous visits here with Miss Dodd and marvelled at the contrast between then and now.

The next day her family came to see her perform. Delighted though she was to see them again, she wished that they had chosen a day when she was not riding for she was quite nervous enough already. All the best lady riders in the country were competing in this preliminary qualifying competition for the Queen Elizabeth Cup, and there was also a French girl who had already won the Cup on a previous occasion and an Italian girl who had last year won the Ladies' European Championship. And yet, looking around at her opponents in the collecting ring, Fiona liked the look of Lucifer far more than any of the other horses.

The course was less straight-forward than it had been the previous morning, for which she was duly thankful. The barrage was to be contested against the clock and the fewer clear rounds there were, she reasoned, the better her chances—always assuming, of course, that she jumped a clear round in the first place.

As luck would have it, she did. Lucifer went like a veteran and never looked nor felt like making a mistake. And, to her unbounded joy, there were only five other clear rounds, with the Italian girl not numbered among them. She was lucky too, in that the competition had been divided into two sections, with most of the outstanding British riders in the second division that was to be jumped later in the day. It seemed that the French girl would be her most serious rival.

Gavin appeared to be too excited by the occasion to offer his customary riding orders. A brief "Good luck", and he turned away and left her to her own devices—but not before she had seen that strange look in his eyes again. "Something is happening," she said to herself, and then tried to dismiss the whole thing from her mind and concentrate upon the job in hand.

She decided to go only as fast as was consistent with extreme caution, even though she was drawn to jump-off first. It was all very well to set a fast standard, she told herself, but not at the expense of a falling pole.

Having decided upon her course of action she resolutely shut her mind to everything else—to the importance of the event, to the crowds in general and the Anstruthers and her parents in particular. Every cell of her brain and every muscle of her body was concentrated upon jumping each fence clearly. When the bell went she set off through the start as if in a trance, feeling like a robot.

It was, she read afterwards in the Press, a copybook round. She made such good use of the ground, too, helped by Lucifer's dressage experience, that her time was good despite the fact that she took no chances. As she rode out of the ring to the echo of "Last competitor—clear round!" over the public address system she knew that, even if she was ultimately to be beaten, she was very far from being disgraced.

She handed the gallant Lucifer over to a jubilant Gavin and together they stood and watched the next rider. She was clearly going for speed, and she hit the last fence for her pains. The third tried for a clear round in slower time, but still had a brick out of the wall. The fourth had a refusal at the spread fence going out of the short-distanced double and the fifth, although clear, was nearly three seconds slower than Lucifer.

It was now or never, thought Fiona, as the French girl galloped into the ring like a meteor on a fiery little liver-chestnut Anglo-Arab. The horse went like the wind and jumped big and cleanly, and he would take a lot of beating. Hating herself for being so unsporting, she nevertheless hoped upon hope that he would make some mistake that would leave Lucifer the victor. Moments later she reproached herself for, amid gasps of disappointment from the stands, the French girl took the wrong course and the bell rang to eliminate her.

Fiona, dumbfounded, stood rooted to the spot.

"Come on!" said Gavin, laughing at her. "Get up and go into the ring. You've won, you know! Oh, well done, Fiona!"

"But I don't like winning like that," Fiona protested.

Gavin looked at her incredulously.

"I'd much sooner have beaten her fair and square," she went on. "This is really winning by default."

She re-mounted and rode back into the ring in a daze. The crowds clapped enthusiastically as the commentator told them that this was a new combination to the ranks of winners. Still unable to believe that she had won, she received her rosette from the gracious hands of a Royal duchess. The French girl smiled and shook her warmly by the hand and she began to feel somewhat better. When she got back to the collecting ring after cantering around the arena to another burst of applause her parents and the Anstruthers were all waiting to embrace her.

"She's an odd girl!" Gavin announced laughingly. "She wishes she hadn't won because she feels it isn't fair! If it were up to her—which thank heaven it isn't—she'd have given the French girl another chance to beat her!"

"It's fair enough, my dear," said the Colonel reassuringly. "That's Show Jumping—the luck of the game. She might not have gone clear and beaten you even if she had finished her round. One day you're up, the next day you're down, at this job. It's partly the element of chance that makes it so fascinating. She's a very good and experienced rider but she can't win all the time. If it'll make you feel any better, she may still win the final to-morrow."

A leading national daily newspaper carried a photograph of Fiona and Lucifer the following day and confidently "tipped" her to win the Queen's Cup. "That's torn it!" remarked Gavin glumly as they read the report together. "I wouldn't give a lot for your chances now. These correspondents are almost invariably wrong in their forecasts."

Fiona knew, however, that she must stand a sporting chance of finishing in the money, at least. The final was to be fought out between the six highest-placed horses in each of the preliminary qualifying sections, and she had beaten five of them already. Word had got around in the collecting ring, via the grape-vine, that the French girl, who was exceedingly superstitious, took the previous day's debacle as a bad omen and was not expecting to win. The leading British lady rider had failed to qualify on her best horse and had just scraped in on a very moderate animal that she was riding for the season for a rich industrialist, and no one expected her to finish in the first three.

The final, however, was to take place at night, and nobody knew just how Lucifer would go under the floodlights.

"If I had only dared to hope that you would get so far, I'd have arranged for a few practices at home," said the Colonel. "Even car headlights would have been better than nothing. Still, we must just take our chance and hope that the fates are with us."

But the fates had evidently already decided that Fiona had had quite as much success as was good for her. Lucifer was definitely "peepy" as he cantered out into the arena and he baulked at the shadow that was thrown across the grass by the narrow stile, took off too late and hit it with his knees. As there were two clear rounds, he finished third without having to jump again. The competition, despite her premonitions to the contrary, was eventually won by the French girl—"So now your conscience is assuaged!" Gavin told Fiona whimsically.

There were no more suitable competitions for Lucifer that week, so as they could not all stay away for very long and the Anstruthers wanted to stay for the rest of the show, Gavin and Fiona drove back to Gloucestershire at the crack of dawn the following morning.

"Mam'selle will be glad to see us," he remarked as they drove along the Great West road. "She hates the responsibility of being left alone to hold the fort."

Fiona was looking dreamily out of the window. "Mmm," she murmured absently. "Sorry—I was just living it all over again. You know, it's funny but now my parents have even come around to the extent of looking on horses with favour! They were thrilled to bits the other night."

"The glamorous side appeals to everyone, and they must have been as proud as Punch to see you winning. So was I, for that matter."

She looked at him in mild surprise. He had never sounded so proprietory before. Then, meeting his eyes and reading the message in them, she felt suddenly shy again.

CHAPTER XII

Clear Last Round

A couple of weeks later an official letter was waiting beside the Colonel's plate when he came down to breakfast. He looked at it and groaned.

"Yet another communication from the British Show Jumping Association," he grunted. "They're forever writing me letters. What on earth can they want this time?"

He slit open the envelope and, pulling out a single sheet of paper, started to read. "Well I'm blessed!" he ejaculated presently.

"Nothing wrong?" asked his wife.

"Wrong? No—quite the reverse. They are getting up a team of promising young horses and riders to go to Rotterdam International Show next month and they've invited Fiona and Lucifer."

Fiona's bottom jaw and her knife dropped simultaneously. "*Me*?—to Rotterdam?" she repeated incredulously.

"That's wonderful!" exclaimed Gavin excitedly. "We must accept, of course. It'll be tremendous fun—and terribly good experience for Lucifer," he added hastily, with an anxious look at his father.

"What do you mean, *we*?" queried the Colonel with the beginning of a smile playing around the corners of his mouth.

"Well, Fiona can't go gallivanting off to the Continent all by herself. She needs an escort and she needs a groom. I'll have to go with her, of course."

"Fiona can't go gallivanting off to the Continent with you either, young man. To begin with, what do you think her parents would say?"

Gavin looked helplessly at Fiona and then turned to his mother, who smiled at him encouragingly. Then he turned back to his father, cleared his throat and said hurriedly:

"Well, father, I have been making plans . . ."

"They had better be good ones," his father remarked, opening his *Times*.

"They are. I love Fiona and I hope she loves me. We want to get married. It might just as well be before Rotterdam as later."

"Bless my soul!" the Colonel was plainly astonished, and equally plainly lost for words. "Did you know about this, my dear?"

"I had a very shrewd suspicion!" admitted his wife. "Isn't it wonderful? I've always wanted a daughter, and I couldn't have chosen a nicer one myself," and Mrs. Anstruther got up and went around the table to Fiona, slipping an arm round her shoulders, and kissed her lightly on the forehead.

"I agree, it's quite splendid! In fact, I never dared hope for anything as good!" beamed her husband. "Now, the first thing for you to do, young man, is to go up to London and see Fiona's parents. I hope that they will be as happy about the arrangement as we are, my dear," and he too arose and kissed his prospective daughter-in-law.

Gavin looked infinitely relieved. "Well, that's that! We'll have our honeymoon in Rotterdam, darling!"

"But what about Lucifer?" protested Fiona weakly, feeling that she was being swept along irresistably by a strong tide.

"That will be one time we can do without him. We'll take one of the girls out to Rotterdam with us and she can bring him home while we stay on."

Fiona's parents thought that their daughter was far too young to think of getting married, but luckily they thoroughly approved of Gavin and, although a little reluctantly, they gave their consent. Mrs. Jamieson's attitude was enormously improved by the fact that Fiona agreed to be married at a fashionable church in London, the ceremony to be followed by a large reception at the Hyde Park Hotel. She enjoyed nothing better than organising this sort of thing, and she threw herself whole-heartedly into the preparations.

Fiona was immediately caught up in a whirl of sending out invitations, compiling wedding-present lists and enduring numerous dreary fittings for her wedding gown and her trousseau. She found it all a little tedious, but as it pleased her parents she submitted gracefully.

"Poor mother," she told Gavin. "She's been longing to do this sort of thing for me ever since I left school. I've been a very disappointing subject for her. The least I can do is to put up with it, much as I detest all the fuss and bother."

"You are a funny girl!" Gavin teased her. "Most of them would positively revel in it! I must say, though, that I'm inclined to agree with you. To a mere man it does seem to be rather much ado about nothing."

"Nothing!" echoed Fiona with an abrupt about-face. "It *is* our wedding, after all! Not very gallant of you to refer to it as 'nothing'!"

"Darling!" he expostulated. "You know I didn't mean anything of the sort! I simply meant that I'd sooner get married quietly, as you would, without any guests at all. We'll live happily ever after, either way."

Much, much later, after a highly social wedding which Fiona had nevertheless enjoyed far more than she had expected to, Miles, who had been best man, drove them out to London Airport en route for Rotterdam and the first stage of their honeymoon.

All their friends had gathered at the hotel entrance to see them off—even Mr. and Mrs. Prendergast and Mr. Brimacombe, who had come all the way up from Devonshire for the wedding, and Miss Dodd, looking quite incongruous in a faded flowered silk frock of a very ancient cut.

And, as they sat in the 'plane side by side, looking down through white wisps of cloud at the silvery Channel far beneath them, Fiona recalled Aunt Helen's last words as her godmother kissed her goodbye.

"I knew I was doing the right thing when I told your parents to send you to Wellesley Hall," she had said smilingly. "But even I did not expect it to turn out quite as happily as this!"

At that point Gavin interrupted her musing by taking her hand.

"Well, Mrs. Anstruther!" he said softly. "This is the beginning. If Lucifer never does anything else for me but bring us together, he has a home with us as long as he lives!"